Betty Crocker's

RED SPOON COLLECTION™

BEST RECIPES FOR

GROUND
MEAT

PRENTICE
HALL
PRESS

New York   London   Toronto   Sydney   Tokyo   Singapore

PRENTICE HALL PRESS
15 Columbus Circle
New York, New York 10023

Copyright © 1991 by General Mills, Inc.,
Minneapolis, Minnesota

Published simultaneously in Canada by Prentice Hall Canada Inc.

PRENTICE HALL PRESS and colophons are registered
trademarks of Simon & Schuster, Inc.

BETTY CROCKER is a registered trademark
of General Mills, Inc.

RED SPOON COLLECTION is a trademark of General Mills, Inc.

Library of Congress Cataloging-in-Publication Data

Best recipes for ground meat.
    p.   cm.—(Betty Crocker's red spoon collection)
  Includes index.
  ISBN 0-13-068354-X
  1. Cookery (Meat) I. Series.
TX749.B414 1991
641.6′6—dc20   90-39876
                                               CIP

Manufactured in the United States of America

10 9 8 7 6 5 4 3 2 1

First Edition

Front Cover: Chili (page 82)

CONTENTS

INTRODUCTION

Ground Meat

Ground meat is the ever-popular answer to the problem of what to make for dinner. Its versatility is astounding, from the variety of meats available—beef, veal, turkey, lamb, pork even buffalo—to the number of ways it can be served. Hamburgers could very well be called America's favorite meal, and everyone seems to have a yen for tacos, meatballs and chili.

A package of ground meat can also be your passport to a world of exotic menus, charting new dinner ideas that may even rival your love of the hamburger. Try Piroshki from Eastern Europe (page 27), Manicotti from Italy (page 59), Moussaka from Greece (pages 68–69), Canadian Pork Pie (page 87), Thai Pork and Pineapple (page 90) and, of course, Swedish Meatballs (page 76).

The original purpose of grinding meat was to extend the number of servings, as well as to utilize less tender and less desirable cuts of meat. This means that most ground meat is an economical way to serve meat, one that gives you all the rich flavor of the meat and allows you to shape and cook it in any number of ways, without the high price tag of a filet or other prime cuts. Ground meat allows a cook's creativity and ingenuity free rein, since it can be shaped or molded, added to pasta, rice, beans or vegetables, encased in pastry, featured in soups and stews, spiced to be hot or mild and to reflect Oriental, Indian, American, Mexican, Mediterranean or European cuisines.

The Red Spoon Tips at the back of this book will give you more information about ground meat, from freezing, storage and cooking tips to suggestions for tonight's dinner.

Ground Beef Guide

The meat most commonly ground is beef, and the different grades are listed below. They range from the least expensive (those with the highest fat content) to the more expensive but leaner ones.

HAMBURGER: The most frequently purchased form of ground beef, it can contain up to 30 percent fat, including added fat not originally part of the piece of beef that has been ground.

GROUND BEEF: The permissible fat content may be as high as 30 percent, however, it must be the fat originally attached to the beef that was ground; no added fat is included.

LEAN GROUND BEEF (Ground Chuck): The fat level is roughly 20 percent for this ground beef.

EXTRA LEAN GROUND BEEF (Ground Round): This type of ground meat has only about 15 percent fat.

Beyond Beef

Other types of meat are ground for cooking and play some of the same roles as beef, but also have some interesting differences.

GROUND TURKEY: An excellent substitute for ground beef when you want to trim fat and calories. Because they don't have the same fat content as ground beef patties, ground turkey patties may become dry, so be sure not to overcook them.

GROUND VEAL: Veal is young beef, and is usually used to add flavor and texture as part of a mixture of other ground meats, as it's an expensive cut.

GROUND PORK: Generally, ground pork is used in sausage making. It can be delightful by itself, or as part of a mixture of other ground meats to which it adds flavor and some fat.

GROUND LAMB: Lamb is a staple in Middle Eastern cooking, and is used for more piquant, exotic-tasting dishes.

GROUND BUFFALO: This noble animal that once covered the plains and fed both native Americans and settlers is no longer in danger of extinction. Buffalo is now ranched commercially, and can often be found in grocery stores. It has a more distinctive taste than ground beef, and can stand robust seasoning. Its fat content is similar to lean ground meat, so be sure not to let burgers become dry in cooking. For a foolproof recipe, try Grilled Jalapeño Buffalo Burgers (page 19).

Ground meat has become a part of our cooking heritage, and has served cooks well with its ease, variety and economy. Whether you are making dinner for a hungry family, cooking an intimate dinner for two or entertaining a large group with a barbecue, ground meat will help you plan the menu.

· 1 ·

BURGERS

Grilled Hamburgers

4 BURGERS

1 pound ground beef
3 tablespoons finely chopped onion, if
    desired
3 tablespoons water
1/2 teaspoon salt
1/4 teaspoon pepper

Mix all ingredients. Shape mixture into 4 patties, each about 3/4 inch thick. Grill patties about 4 inches from medium coals, 7 to 8 minutes on each side for medium, turning once, to desired doneness. Brush barbecue sauce on patties before and after turning, if desired.

Favorite Burgers

6 BURGERS

1 1/2 pounds ground beef
2 slices bread, torn into small pieces
1/3 cup milk
1/4 cup ketchup
1 small onion, finely chopped (about
    1/4 cup)
1 teaspoon salt
2 teaspoons horseradish
2 teaspoons Worcestershire sauce
1 tablespoon prepared mustard

Mix all ingredients. Shape mixture into 6 patties, about 3/4 inch thick. Broil or grill about 4 inches from heat, 7 to 8 minutes on each side for medium, turning once, to desired doneness.

Following pages: Grilled Hamburgers

7

Zesty Burgers

1 pound ground beef
⅓ cup dry bread crumbs
½ cup water
1 teaspoon instant beef bouillon
1 teaspoon grated lemon peel
1 teaspoon lemon juice
½ teaspoon salt
½ teaspoon ground sage
½ teaspoon ground ginger
¼ teaspoon pepper

Mix all ingredients. Shape mixture into 4 patties, about ¾ inch thick. Broil or grill about 4 inches from heat, 7 to 8 minutes on each side for medium, turning once, to desired doneness.

Chili-Cheese Burgers

1½ pounds ground beef
1 small onion, finely chopped (about ¼ cup)
1 teaspoon chili powder
1 teaspoon Worcestershire sauce
¾ teaspoon salt
¼ teaspoon garlic salt
¼ teaspoon pepper
¼ teaspoon red pepper sauce
Dash cayenne red pepper
6 slices Cheddar cheese, 2 × 2 inches
2 tablespoons canned chopped green chilies

Mix all ingredients except cheese and chilies. Shape mixture into 12 thin patties, about 3½ inches in diameter. Place 1 cheese slice and 1 teaspoon chilies on each of 6 patties. Top with a remaining patty, sealing edges firmly. Broil or grill patties about 4 inches from heat, 7 to 8 minutes on each side for medium, turning once, to desired doneness.

Blue Ribbon Burgers

2 pounds ground beef
2 teaspoons Worcestershire sauce
1/2 teaspoon salt
1/4 teaspoon garlic salt
1/4 teaspoon pepper
1 package (3 ounces) cream cheese,
* softened*
2 tablespoons crumbled blue cheese
1 can (4 ounces) mushroom stems and
* pieces, drained and chopped*

Mix meat, Worcestershire sauce and seasonings. Shape mixture into 12 thin patties, about 4 inches in diameter.

Mix cream cheese and blue cheese. Top each of 6 patties with cheese mixture, spreading to within 1/2 inch of edge; press mushrooms into cheese. Cover each with a remaining patty, sealing edges firmly. Broil or grill patties about 4 inches from heat, 7 to 8 minutes on each side for medium, turning once, to desired doneness.

Savory Mushroom Hamburgers

2 tablespoons margarine or butter
1 teaspoon Worcestershire sauce
1/4 teaspoon lemon juice
1 clove garlic, minced
1 small onion, sliced
1 cup washed, trimmed sliced
* mushrooms**
1 pound lean ground beef
1/2 teaspoon salt
1/4 teaspoon pepper

Melt margarine in large skillet. Add Worcestershire sauce, lemon juice, garlic, onion and mushrooms; cook and stir over medium heat 2 minutes. Remove from heat.

Mix meat, salt and pepper. Shape mixture into 4 patties, about 3/4 inch thick. Push mushroom-onion mixture to side of skillet. Cook patties in same skillet over medium-high heat, about 10 minutes, turning once, to desired doneness. Serve mushroom-onion mixture over patties.

*You can substitute 1/2 cup drained, canned sliced mushrooms for the fresh mushrooms.

Marinated Blue Cheese Burgers

6 BURGERS

1 cup dry red wine
1½ pounds ground beef
½ cup crushed buttery cracker crumbs
 (about 12 crackers)
¼ cup sliced green onions (with tops)
2 tablespoons crumbled blue cheese
 (1 ounce)
¼ teaspoon pepper
6 slices bacon

Remove 2 tablespoons wine for patties; reserve remaining wine for marinating. Mix 2 tablespoons wine and the remaining ingredients except bacon and reserved wine. Shape into 6 oval patties, each about 1¼ inches thick.

Wrap 1 slice bacon around each patty and secure with wooden pick. Arrange patties in shallow glass or plastic dish. Pour reserved wine over patties; cover. Refrigerate, turning once, at least 6 hours but no longer than 24 hours.

Remove patties from wine and broil or grill about 4 inches from heat, 7 to 8 minutes on each side for medium, turning once to desired doneness. Serve with additional crumbled blue cheese, if desired.

Southwest Burgers

6 BURGERS

1½ pounds ground beef
1 can (4 ounces) chopped green chilies,
 drained
½ cup diced Monterey Jack cheese
½ teaspoon pepper
¼ teaspoon salt
Salsa

Mix all ingredients except salsa. Shape into 6 patties, each about ½ inch thick. Broil with tops of burgers about 4 inches from heat, 7 to 8 minutes on each side for medium, turning once, to desired doneness. Serve with salsa.

Hamburgers Parmigiana

1 pound ground beef
1 small onion, chopped (about ¼ cup)
2 tablespoons grated Parmesan cheese
½ teaspoon garlic salt
1 jar (15 ounces) chunky spaghetti sauce
½ cup shredded mozzarella cheese
4 slices French bread, toasted, or 2
  hamburger buns, split and toasted

Mix ground beef, onion, Parmesan cheese and garlic salt. Shape into 4 patties, each about ½ inch thick. Cook in 10-inch skillet over medium heat, turning frequently, to desired doneness; drain.

Pour spaghetti sauce over patties; heat until hot. Top each patty with 2 tablespoons mozzarella cheese; let stand until cheese begins to melt. Serve on French bread.

Grilled Deviled Burgers

1 pound ground beef
1 can (4¼ ounces) deviled ham
1 small onion, finely chopped (about
  ¼ cup)
¼ teaspoon salt
⅛ teaspoon garlic salt
⅛ teaspoon pepper
1 can (8 ounces) sauerkraut, drained
5 slices Swiss cheese, 3 × 3 inches

Mix all ingredients except sauerkraut and cheese. Shape mixture into 5 patties, each about ¾ inch thick. Grill patties about 4 inches from medium coals 3 minutes; turn patties and top each with sauerkraut and cheese slice. Grill to desired doneness, 2 to 4 minutes longer for medium. Serve on toasted rye or pumpernickel buns, if desired.

TO MICROWAVE: Prepare patties as directed above. Arrange patties on microwavable rack in microwavable dish. Cover with waxed paper and microwave on high 3 minutes; rotate dish ½ turn. Microwave until patties are almost done, 2 to 4 minutes longer. Pour off drippings.

Top each patty with sauerkraut and cheese slice. Microwave uncovered 1 minute; rotate dish ½ turn. Microwave until cheese begins to melt, 30 to 90 seconds longer. Serve on toasted rye or pumpernickel buns, if desired.

Taco Patties

1 1/2 pounds ground beef
1 small onion, chopped (about 1/4 cup)
1 teaspoon salt
1 teaspoon Worcestershire sauce
1/4 teaspoon pepper
3/4 cup water
1 envelope (about 1 1/4 ounces) taco
  seasoning mix
1 ripe small avocado*
1 cup shredded Cheddar cheese (4 ounces)

Mix meat, onion, salt, Worcestershire sauce and pepper. Shape mixture into 6 patties, about 3/4 inch thick. Brown patties in large skillet over medium-high heat, turning once. Remove patties and set aside. Pour fat from skillet.

Mix water and seasoning mix in same skillet; heat to boiling, stirring constantly. Reduce heat; return patties to skillet and turn each to coat with sauce.

Peel avocado and cut into 6 slices. Top each patty with an avocado slice, cover and simmer 10 minutes. Sprinkle with cheese; cover and heat until cheese is melted, about 2 minutes. Serve sauce over patties.

*You can substitute 1 medium tomato, sliced, for the avocado slices.

Grilled Teriyaki Burgers

4 BURGERS

1 pound ground beef
2 tablespoons soy sauce
1 teaspoon salt
1/4 teaspoon crushed gingerroot or
  1/8 teaspoon ground ginger
1 clove garlic, crushed

Shape ground beef into 4 patties, each about 3/4 inch thick. Mix remaining ingredients; spoon onto patties. Turn patties; let stand 10 minutes.

Grill patties about 4 inches from medium coals, 7 to 8 minutes on each side for medium, turning once, to desired doneness. Serve on toasted sesame seed buns, if desired.

TO BROIL: Prepare patties as directed above. Set oven control to broil. Place patties on rack in broiler pan. Broil with tops about 4 inches from heat, 7 to 8 minutes on each side for medium, turning once, to desired doneness. Serve on toasted sesame seed buns, if desired.

Broiled Burgers with Mushrooms and Onions

1 pound ground beef
3 tablespoons finely chopped onion
3 tablespoons water
¾ teaspoon salt
⅛ teaspoon pepper
Mushrooms and Onions (below)

Mix ground beef, onion, water, salt and pepper. Shape mixture into 4 patties, each about ¾ inch thick.

Set oven control to broil. Place patties on rack in broiler pan. Broil with tops about 4 inches from heat 7 to 8 minutes on each side for medium, turning once, to desired doneness. Prepare Mushrooms and Onions; spoon over hamburgers.

MUSHROOMS AND ONIONS

1 medium onion, thinly sliced
1 tablespoon margarine or butter
4 ounces sliced fresh mushrooms (about ¼ cup)
½ teaspoon Worcestershire sauce

Cook onion and mushrooms in margarine over medium heat, stirring occasionally, until tender; stir in Worcestershire sauce.

TO GRILL: Prepare patties as directed above. Grill as directed for Grilled Hamburgers (page 7). Serve as directed above.

TO MICROWAVE: Prepare patties as directed above. Place patties on microwavable rack in microwavable dish. Cover with waxed paper and microwave on high 3 minutes; rotate dish ½ turn. Microwave until almost done, about 2 minutes longer. Let stand covered 3 minutes.

Place onion and margarine in 1-quart microwavable casserole. Cover tightly and microwave on high until onion is crisp-tender, about 2 minutes. Stir in mushrooms and Worcestershire sauce. Cover tightly and microwave until mushrooms are hot, about 1 minute. Spoon over hamburgers.

Following pages: Broiled Burgers with Mushrooms and Onions

Barbecue Hamburger Patties

6 BURGERS

1½ pounds ground beef
1 medium onion, chopped (about ½ cup)
1 teaspoon salt
⅓ cup ketchup
⅓ cup chili sauce
2 tablespoons brown sugar
1 tablespoon lemon juice

Mix beef, onion and salt. Shape mixture into 6 patties, about ¾ inch thick. Brown patties in large skillet over medium-high heat, turning once. Cover and cook over low heat 10 minutes. Drain off fat.

Mix ketchup, chili sauce, brown sugar and lemon juice; pour over patties. Cover and simmer 15 minutes, spooning sauce onto patties occasionally. Serve the sauce over patties.

Scandinavian Hamburgers

4 BURGERS

1 pound ground beef
1 egg
½ cup cold mashed potatoes
½ teaspoon salt
¼ teaspoon pepper
¼ cup finely chopped pickled beets
2 tablespoons finely chopped onion
2 tablespoons capers

Mix beef, egg, potatoes, salt and pepper. Stir in remaining ingredients. Shape mixture into 4 patties, each about 1 inch thick. Broil or grill patties about 4 inches from heat, 7 to 8 minutes on each side for medium, turning once, to desired doneness. Top each patty with fried egg, if desired.

Burgundy Burgers

6 BURGERS

1½ pounds ground beef
¼ cup Burgundy or other red wine
1 small onion, finely chopped (about
  ¼ cup)
1 tablespoon Worcestershire sauce
1 teaspoon seasoned salt
¼ teaspoon pepper
⅛ teaspoon garlic salt

Mix all ingredients. Shape mixture into 6 patties, about ¾ inch thick. Broil or grill patties about 4 inches from heat, 7 to 8 minutes on each side for medium, turning once, to desired doneness.

Grilled Coney Island Burgers

6 BURGERS

1 pound ground beef
½ can (15 ounces) chili with beans
1 tablespoon chopped green chilies
6 frankfurter buns, split and warmed

Shape ground beef into 6 rolls, each about 5 inches long and ¾ inch thick. Mix chili and green chilies in small grill pan; heat on grill until hot.

Grill ground beef rolls about 4 inches from medium coals, 3 to 5 minutes on each side for medium, turning once, to desired doneness. Serve in frankfurter buns; spoon about 2 tablespoons chili mixture into each bun.

TO BROIL: Mix chili and green chilies in saucepan; heat until hot. Prepare ground beef rolls as directed above. Broil with tops about 4 inches from heat, about 3 minutes on each side for medium, turning once, to desired doneness. Serve as directed above.

Grilled Jalapeño Buffalo Burgers

6 BURGERS

1½ pounds ground buffalo or ground beef
1 medium onion, finely chopped (about ½ cup)
2 to 3 jalapeño chilies, seeded and finely chopped
1 clove garlic, finely chopped
Chili sauce or salsa

Mix all ingredients except for chili sauce. Shape into 6 patties, each about ½ inch thick.

Brush grill with vegetable oil. Grill patties about 4 inches from medium coals, 7 to 8 minutes on each side for medium, turning once, to desired doneness. Serve with chili sauce.

BROILED JALAPEÑO BUFFALO BURGERS: Set oven control to broil. Place patties on rack in broiler pan. Broil with tops about 4 inches from heat, 7 to 8 minutes on each side for medium, turning once, to desired doneness.

· 2 ·

SANDWICHES, SOUPS
AND STEWS

Sloppy Joes

1 pound ground beef
1 medium onion, chopped (about ½ cup)
⅓ cup chopped celery
⅓ cup chopped green pepper
⅓ cup ketchup
¼ cup water
1 tablespoon Worcestershire sauce
½ teaspoon salt
⅛ teaspoon red pepper sauce
6 hamburger buns, split and toasted

Cook and stir ground beef and onion in 10-inch skillet until beef is brown; drain. Stir in remaining ingredients except buns. Cover and cook over low heat just until vegetables are tender, 10 to 15 minutes. Fill buns with beef mixture.

Sloppy Joes with Cabbage

1 pound ground beef
1 medium onion, chopped (about ½ cup)
½ cup thinly sliced celery
2 cups shredded cabbage
⅓ cup chopped green pepper
¾ cup ketchup
¼ cup water
¼ teaspoon salt
1 tablespoon prepared mustard
8 hamburger buns, split and toasted

Cook and stir meat, onion and celery in large skillet until meat is brown. Drain off fat. Stir in cabbage, green pepper, ketchup, water, salt and mustard; heat to boiling, stirring occasionally. Reduce heat; cover and simmer until vegetables are tender, about 25 minutes. Spoon mixture onto bottom halves of buns; top with remaining halves.

Sloppy Joes with Potatoes and Onion

4 SERVINGS

1 pound lean ground beef
Salt and pepper to taste
1 medium onion, sliced and separated
  into rings
2 medium potatoes, thinly sliced
1 can (15½ ounces) Sloppy Joe sauce

Crumble ground beef into 10-inch skillet; sprinkle with salt and pepper. Layer onion and potatoes on beef; pour sauce over top.

Cover and cook over low heat until beef is done and potatoes are tender, about 30 minutes.

TO MICROWAVE: Crumble ground beef into 2-quart microwavable casserole; sprinkle with salt and pepper. Layer onion and potatoes on beef. Cover tightly and microwave on high 5 minutes; rotate casserole ½ turn. Microwave 5 minutes longer.

Stir 1 teaspoon sugar into sauce; pour sauce over potatoes. Cover tightly and microwave 5 minutes; rotate casserole ½ turn. Microwave until potatoes are tender, 5 to 6 minutes longer.

Tacos

8 TO 10 TACOS

MEAT FILLING

1 pound ground beef
1 medium onion, chopped (about ½ cup)
1 can (15 ounces) tomato sauce
1 teaspoon garlic salt
½ to 1 teaspoon chili powder
Dash pepper

Cook and stir meat and onion in skillet until meat is brown. Drain off fat. Stir in tomato sauce, garlic salt, chili powder and pepper; simmer uncovered 15 minutes.

While Meat Filling is simmering, heat taco shells as directed on package. Spoon Meat Filling into taco shells. Top filling with cheese, lettuce and tomato. Serve with taco sauce, if desired.

SHELLS AND TOPPINGS

8 to 10 taco shells
1 cup shredded Cheddar cheese (4 ounces)
1 cup shredded lettuce
1 large tomato, chopped

Following pages: Tacos

Oriental Sandwich

1 pound ground beef
1 medium onion, thinly sliced
²/₃ cup water
2 tablespoons cornstarch
3 tablespoons soy sauce
1 tablespoon molasses
¼ teaspoon ginger
1 can (16 ounces) bean sprouts, rinsed
　　and drained
1 can (8 ounces) water chestnuts, drained
　　and sliced
8 hamburger buns, split and toasted

Cook and stir meat and onion in large skillet until onion is tender. Drain off fat. Mix water, cornstarch, soy sauce, molasses and ginger; stir into meat mixture. Add bean sprouts and water chestnuts. Cook, stirring constantly, until mixture thickens and boils, about 5 minutes. Serve on buns and pass additional soy sauce.

Hamburger Pasties

1 pound ground beef
1 small onion, chopped (about ¼ cup)
1 can (8 ounces) peas, drained*
1 medium potato, pared and shredded
1 cup shredded process American or
　　Cheddar cheese (4 ounces)
¼ cup ketchup
½ teaspoon garlic salt
¼ teaspoon pepper
1 tablespoon prepared mustard
1 package (11 ounces) pie crust mix or
　　sticks

Heat oven to 375°. Cook and stir meat and onion in large skillet until meat is brown. Drain off fat. Remove from heat; stir in remaining ingredients except pie crust mix and set aside.

Prepare pastry for Two-Crust Pie as directed on package. Divide dough into 8 equal parts. Roll each part on floured surface into a 7-inch circle. On half of each circle, spread about ½ cup meat mixture (packed) to within ½ inch of edge. Moisten edge of pastry with water. Fold pastry over filling, sealing edges with fork. Place on ungreased baking sheet; prick tops with fork.

Bake 30 to 35 minutes. You can serve these as sandwiches or, if you prefer, place on plates and top with a favorite gravy or sauce.

*You can substitute 1 cup of a favorite vegetable for the canned peas.

Souper Baked Sandwich

1½ pounds ground beef
1 small onion, chopped (about ¼ cup)
½ cup chopped celery
½ teaspoon salt
4 cups herb-seasoned stuffing cubes
1½ cups milk
2 eggs
1 can (10¾ ounces) condensed cream of
mushroom soup
1 teaspoon dry mustard
1 cup shredded Cheddar cheese (4 ounces)

Heat oven to 350°. Cook and stir meat, onion and celery in large skillet until meat is brown. Drain off fat. Stir in salt.

Arrange stuffing cubes in greased baking pan, 9 × 9 × 2 or 11¾ × 7½ × 1¾ inches; top with meat mixture. Beat milk, eggs, soup and mustard; pour over meat and sprinkle with cheese. Bake uncovered until knife inserted in center comes out clean, 30 to 40 minutes. Cool 5 minutes, then cut into squares.

Hamburger Pizza

CRUST

2½ cups variety baking mix
1 package active dry yeast
⅔ cup hot water

MEAT MIXTURE

1 pound ground beef
1 medium onion, chopped (about ½ cup)
1 can (15 ounces) tomato sauce
2 teaspoons oregano leaves
¼ teaspoon pepper

TOPPING

½ cup chopped green pepper, if desired
2 cups shredded Cheddar or mozzarella
cheese (8 ounces)
1 cup grated Parmesan cheese

Heat oven to 425°. Mix baking mix and yeast; stir in water and beat vigorously. Turn dough onto well-floured surface; knead until smooth, about 20 times. Let dough rest a few minutes.

While dough is resting, cook and stir meat and onion in large skillet until onion is tender. Drain off fat. Stir in tomato sauce, oregano leaves and pepper; set aside.

Divide dough in half. Roll each half on un-greased baking sheet into rectangle, 13 × 10 inches, or in pizza pan into 12-inch circle. Pinch edges to make a slight rim. Spread Meat Mixture almost to edges. Top with green pepper and cheeses. Bake until crust is brown and filling is hot and bubbly, 15 to 20 minutes. Cut into squares or wedges.

Baked Pizza Sandwich

1 pound ground beef
1 can (15 ounces) tomato sauce
1 teaspoon oregano leaves
2 cups variety baking mix
1 egg
2/3 cup milk
1 package (8 ounces) sliced process
    American or mozzarella cheese
1 jar (2 1/2 ounces) sliced mushrooms,
    drained
1/4 cup grated Parmesan cheese

Heat oven to 400°. Cook and stir meat in large skillet until brown. Drain off fat. Stir half the tomato sauce and the oregano leaves into meat; heat to boiling. Reduce heat and simmer uncovered 10 minutes.

While meat mixture is simmering, mix baking mix, egg and milk. Measure ¾ cup of the batter and set aside. Spread remaining batter in greased baking pan, 9 × 9 × 2 inches. Pour remaining tomato sauce over batter, spreading it evenly. Layer 4 slices cheese, the meat mixture, mushrooms and remaining cheese slices on batter. Spoon reserved batter on top. Sprinkle with Parmesan cheese. Bake uncovered until golden brown, 20 to 25 minutes. Cool 5 minutes, then cut into squares.

Chiliburgers in Crusts

1 1/2 pounds ground beef
1 can (8 ounces) whole kernel corn,
    drained
1 can (4 ounces) chopped green chilies,
    drained
2 teaspoons chili powder
1 teaspoon salt
2 1/3 cups variety baking mix
3 tablespoons margarine or butter, melted
1/2 cup milk

Mix ground beef, corn, chilies, chili powder and salt. Shape mixture into 6 patties; place on rack in broiler pan. Set oven control to broil and/or 550°. Broil with tops 3 to 4 inches from heat 4 minutes on each side.

Mix remaining ingredients until soft dough forms and beat vigorously 20 strokes. Gently smooth dough into ball on floured cloth-covered board. Knead 5 times. Roll ⅛ inch thick. Cut out 12 rounds with floured 4½-inch biscuit cutter. Place beef patties on 6 of the rounds; top each with another round. Pinch edges together to seal. Place on ungreased cookie sheet, and bake in 400° oven until golden brown, about 15 minutes.

Piroshki

1 pound ground beef
1 medium onion, chopped (about ½ cup)
½ cup shredded Cheddar cheese
½ teaspoon salt
⅛ teaspoon pepper
2 cups variety baking mix
½ cup cold water
Margarine or butter, melted
Chili sauce or ketchup

Heat oven to 450°. Cook and stir ground beef and onion until brown; drain. Stir in cheese, salt and pepper. Mix baking mix and cold water until soft dough forms; beat vigorously 20 strokes. Gently smooth dough into ball on floured cloth-covered board. Knead 5 times. Roll dough into 16-inch square; cut into 4 squares.

Place 1 cup beef mixture in center of each square. Bring opposite corners together at center to form triangles. Pinch edges together to seal securely, making 4 diagonal seams. Brush with margarine. Place on ungreased cookie sheet, and bake in 450° oven until golden brown, about 10 minutes. Serve with chili sauce.

Sausage Burritos

1 package (12 ounces) bulk seasoned pork
*   sausage*
1 medium onion, sliced
1 medium green pepper, cut into ¼-inch
*   strips*
6 flour tortillas (10 inches in diameter)
1 can (16 ounces) baked beans in
*   molasses*
½ head lettuce, shredded (about 3 cups)

Cook and stir pork, onion and green pepper over medium heat until pork is done, about 10 minutes; drain. Prepare tortillas as directed on package. Spoon about 3 tablespoons beans down center of each tortilla. Divide sausage mixture among tortillas. Top with lettuce.

Spicy Lamb in Pita Breads

4 SANDWICHES

Yogurt Dressing (below)
1 pound ground lamb
1 small onion, chopped (about 1/4 cup)
1 clove garlic, crushed
1 tablespoon vegetable oil
1/2 teaspoon salt
1/2 teaspoon ground cumin
1/4 teaspoon pepper
4 whole wheat pita breads (6 inches in
    diameter)
Shredded lettuce
1 medium tomato, chopped

Prepare Yogurt Dressing. Cook and stir ground lamb, onion and garlic in oil over medium heat until lamb is brown; drain. Stir in salt, cumin and pepper.

Split each pita bread halfway around the edge with knife; separate to form pocket. Spoon one-fourth of the lamb mixture into each pocket. Top with lettuce and tomato. Serve with Yogurt Dressing.

YOGURT DRESSING

1/2 cup plain yogurt
1 tablespoon snipped fresh mint leaves or
    1 teaspoon dried mint leaves
1 teaspoon sugar
1/4 small cucumber, seeded and chopped

Mix all ingredients; cover and refrigerate.

Mexican Soup

6 SERVINGS

1 pound ground beef
1/4 cup chopped green pepper
1 medium onion, chopped (about 1/2 cup)
5 cups water
1 teaspoon chili powder
1/2 teaspoon garlic salt
1/4 teaspoon salt
1 can (16 ounces) whole tomatoes,
    undrained
1 package (7.5 ounces) main dish mix for
    chili tomato
1 can (8 ounces) whole kernel corn,
    undrained
2 tablespoons sliced pitted ripe olives

Cook and stir ground beef, green pepper and onion in Dutch oven until beef is brown; drain. Stir in water, chili powder, garlic salt, salt, tomatoes and Sauce Mix; break up tomatoes with fork. Heat to boiling, stirring constantly; reduce heat. Cover and simmer, stirring occasionally, 10 minutes. Stir in Macaroni, corn and olives. Cover and cook 10 minutes longer. Garnish with corn chips, if desired.

Beef-Vegetable Soup

1 pound ground beef
2 medium stalks celery, sliced (about
  1 cup)
1 large onion, chopped (about 1 cup)
1 can (16 ounces) whole tomatoes
1 can (16 ounces) diced beets
1 can (16 ounces) sliced carrots, drained
1 tablespoon instant beef bouillon
2 teaspoons snipped parsley
1 teaspoon salt
1/2 teaspoon ground nutmeg
1 can (12 ounces) beer
2 cups shredded cabbage

Cook and stir beef, celery and onion in 4-quart Dutch oven until beef is light brown; drain. Stir in tomatoes (with liquid), beets (with liquid), carrots, bouillon (dry), parsley, salt and nutmeg; break up tomatoes with fork. Heat to boiling; reduce heat. Cover and simmer 10 minutes. Stir in beer and cabbage. Heat to boiling; reduce heat. Cover and simmer until cabbage is crisp-tender, about 5 minutes.

Hamburger Minestrone

2 pounds ground beef
1 large onion, chopped (about 1 cup)
1 clove garlic, finely chopped
2 cups beef broth
1/2 cup red wine or water
1 cup uncooked elbow macaroni or broken
  spaghetti
2 cups shredded cabbage
2 small zucchini, sliced (about 2 cups)
2 stalks celery, sliced (about 1 cup)
1 1/2 teaspoons Italian seasoning
1 teaspoon salt
1 can (28 ounces) whole tomatoes,
  undrained
1 can (15 ounces) kidney beans,
  undrained
1 can (11 ounces) vacuum pack whole
  kernel corn, undrained
Grated Parmesan cheese

Cook and stir ground beef, onion and garlic in Dutch oven until beef is brown; drain. Stir in remaining ingredients except cheese; break up tomatoes with fork. Heat to boiling; reduce heat. Cover and simmer, stirring occasionally, until macaroni and vegetables are tender, about 30 minutes. Serve with cheese.

Following pages: Spicy Lamb in Pita Breads

Tortellini and Sausage Soup

1 pound bulk Italian sausage
1 medium onion, coarsely chopped (about
  1/2 cup)
3 cups water
1/2 teaspoon dried basil leaves
1/2 teaspoon dried oregano leaves
2 carrots, sliced
1 medium zucchini or yellow summer
  squash, halved and sliced
2 cans (10³/4 ounces each) condensed
  tomato soup
8 ounces uncooked dried or frozen cheese-
  or meat-filled tortellini (2 cups)
Grated Parmesan cheese

Cook and stir sausage and onion in 4-quart Dutch oven until sausage is light brown; drain. Stir in remaining ingredients except cheese.

Heat to boiling; reduce heat. Cover and simmer until vegetables and tortellini are tender, about 20 minutes. Serve with cheese.

GARBANZO BEAN AND SAUSAGE SOUP: Substitute 1 can (15 ounces) garbanzo beans, drained, for the tortellini.

Beef and Bulgur Stew

1¹/2 pounds ground beef
1 medium onion, chopped (about ¹/2 cup)
2 cups water
1 cup uncooked bulgur
1 tablespoon snipped mint leaves or
  1 teaspoon dried mint leaves
1¹/2 teaspoons salt
1 teaspoon dried oregano leaves
1 small eggplant (about 1 pound), cut into
  1-inch pieces
¹/4 cup grated Parmesan cheese
2 medium tomatoes, chopped (about
  1¹/2 cups)

Cook and stir ground beef and onion in Dutch oven until beef is brown; drain. Stir in water, bulgur, mint, salt, oregano and eggplant. Heat to boiling; reduce heat. Cover and simmer, stirring occasionally, until wheat is tender, about 30 minutes (add small amount of water if necessary). Stir in cheese and tomatoes. Heat just until tomatoes are hot, about 5 minutes. Serve with additional cheese, if desired.

Meatball Stew

1 pound ground beef
1/2 cup dry bread crumbs
1/4 cup milk
2 tablespoons finely chopped onion
1/2 teaspoon salt
1/2 teaspoon Worcestershire sauce
1 egg
Seasoning Mix (below)
1 1/2 cups water
4 medium stalks celery, cut into 1/4-inch
  slices (about 2 cups)
1 can (16 ounces) whole tomatoes,
  undrained
1 can (16 ounces) kidney beans,
  undrained

Mix ground beef, bread crumbs, milk, onion, salt, Worcestershire sauce and egg; shape into eighteen 1 1/2-inch balls. Cook in Dutch oven over medium heat, turning occasionally, until brown, about 10 minutes. Stir in Seasoning Mix until meatballs are coated. Add water, celery, tomatoes and kidney beans. Heat to boiling, stirring frequently. Reduce heat; cover and simmer 30 minutes, stirring occasionally. Add additional water if necessary.

SEASONING MIX

1/4 cup all-purpose flour
2 tablespoons instant minced onion
1 tablespoon instant beef bouillon
1/2 teaspoon salt
1/2 teaspoon garlic powder
1/2 teaspoon chili powder
1/2 teaspoon ground thyme
1/2 teaspoon dried basil leaves
1/8 teaspoon ground marjoram

Combine all ingredients.

Following pages: Tortellini and Sausage Soup

Jiffy Hamburger Stew

4 SERVINGS

1 pound ground beef
2 cups diced potatoes
2 medium onions, chopped (about
   1 cup)
2 teaspoons salt
1/8 teaspoon pepper
1 can (16 ounces) whole tomatoes,
   undrained
Snipped parsley

Cook and stir ground beef, potatoes and onions in 12-inch skillet until beef is brown and onion is tender. Drain fat. Stir in salt, pepper and tomatoes; break up tomatoes with fork. Heat to boiling; reduce heat. Cover and simmer, stirring occasionally, until potatoes are tender, 5 to 10 minutes. Garnish with parsley.

Pocket Stew

4 SERVINGS

1 1/2 pounds ground beef
4 slices Bermuda or Spanish onion
4 cooked, pared medium potatoes
4 medium carrots, cut into julienne strips
1 teaspoon salt
1/8 teaspoon pepper

Heat oven to 400°. Shape meat into 4 patties, each about 3 inches in diameter and 1 inch thick. Place patties on 25 × 18-inch piece of heavy-duty aluminum foil. Top each patty with an onion slice and a potato. Arrange carrots around meat. Season with salt and pepper. Fold foil over potatoes and carrots; seal foil securely.

Place foil package on ungreased baking sheet. Bake until carrots are tender, about 45 minutes.

Note: If you wish to serve individual portions, divide ingredients among 4 foil packets.

Cabbage Patch Stew

1 pound ground beef
2 medium onions, thinly sliced
1½ cups coarsely chopped cabbage
½ cup diced celery
1 can (16 ounces) tomatoes
1 teaspoon garlic salt
1 teaspoon marjoram
½ teaspoon salt
⅛ teaspoon pepper
1 can (15½ ounces) kidney beans,
  undrained
2 cups mashed potatoes

Cook and stir meat in Dutch oven until light brown. Spoon off fat. Add onions, cabbage and celery; cook and stir until vegetables are light brown. Stir in tomatoes and seasonings. Cover tightly; simmer 15 minutes.

Stir in beans (with liquid); heat until mixture boils. Simmer uncovered 15 to 20 minutes. Top stew with mashed potatoes.

Beef and Lentil Stew

6 SERVINGS

1 pound ground beef
1 medium onion, chopped (about ½ cup)
1 clove garlic, minced
1 can (4 ounces) mushroom stems and
  pieces, undrained
1 can (16 ounces) stewed tomatoes
1 stalk celery, sliced
1 large carrot, sliced
1 cup uncooked lentils
3 cups water
¼ cup red wine, if desired
1 bay leaf
2 tablespoons snipped parsley
1 teaspoon salt
1 teaspoon instant beef bouillon
¼ teaspoon pepper

Cook and stir meat, onion and garlic in Dutch oven until meat is brown. Drain off fat. Stir in mushrooms (with liquid) and remaining ingredients; heat to boiling. Reduce heat; cover and simmer, stirring occasionally, until lentils are tender, about 40 minutes. Remove bay leaf.

Following pages: Cabbage Patch Stew

Barley-Beef Stew

1 1/2 *pounds ground beef*
1 *large onion, chopped (about 1 cup)*
2 *stalks celery, sliced (about 1 cup)*
1 *can (28 ounces) whole tomatoes,*
  undrained
2 1/2 *cups water*
1 *cup uncooked barley*
1 *tablespoon chili powder*
3/4 *teaspoon salt*
1/4 *teaspoon pepper*

Cook and stir ground beef, onion and celery in 4-quart Dutch oven over medium heat until beef is brown; drain. Stir in remaining ingredients. Break up tomatoes with fork. Heat to boiling; reduce heat. Cover and simmer until barley is done and stew is desired consistency, about 1 hour.

Italian Chili with Dumplings

1 *package (9 ounces) frozen Italian*
  green beans
1 *pound ground beef*
1 *pound bulk pork sausage*
2 *large onions, chopped (about 2 cups)*
1 *cup chopped green pepper*
4 *cloves garlic, crushed*
3 *medium zucchini, cut into* 1/2-*inch pieces*
  (about 3 cups)
2 *cans (15 ounces each) tomato sauce*
1 *can (16 ounces) whole tomatoes,*
  undrained
1 *tablespoon Italian seasoning*
1 *teaspoon salt*
1/4 *teaspoon pepper*
2 *cups variety baking mix*
1 1/2 *teaspoons Italian seasoning*
2/3 *cup milk*
2 *tablespoons grated Parmesan cheese*
Paprika

Rinse beans under running cold water to separate; drain. Cook and stir ground beef, sausage, onion, green pepper and garlic in Dutch oven until beef is brown; drain. Stir beans, zucchini, tomato sauce, tomatoes (with liquid), 1 tablespoon Italian seasoning, the salt and pepper into beef mixture. Heat to boiling, stirring occasionally; reduce heat. Simmer uncovered, stirring occasionally, 30 minutes.

Mix baking mix, 1 1/2 teaspoons Italian seasoning and the milk until soft dough forms. Drop by spoonfuls into hot stew; sprinkle with cheese and paprika. Cook uncovered over low heat 10 minutes; cover and cook 10 minutes longer.

· 3 ·

LOW-CALORIE DINNERS

Meat Loaf with Green Beans

6 SERVINGS

½ cup soft bread crumbs
⅔ cup skim milk
1 egg
1¼ teaspoons salt
1 pound lean ground beef
1 medium onion, finely chopped (about ½ cup)
1 cup finely shredded carrot
¼ cup finely chopped green pepper
⅓ cup chili sauce
1 can (8 ounces) cut green beans, undrained
1 can (8 ounces) cut wax beans, undrained
Lemon pepper
½ cup chili sauce

Heat oven to 350°. Coat a 5-cup ring mold or loaf pan, 8½ × 4½ × 2¾ inches, with vegetable spray-on for cookware. Mix bread crumbs, skim milk, egg, salt, meat, onion, carrot, green pepper and ⅓ cup chili sauce thoroughly. Spread mixture in ring mold. Bake until done, about 1 hour. Drain off fat.

Heat green and wax beans (with liquid) to boiling; drain. Season with lemon pepper. Loosen meat from side of mold; unmold onto serving platter. Spread ½ cup chili sauce on top; spoon beans into center of ring or around loaf.

Zucchini Lasagne

1 pound lean ground beef
1 can (15 ounces) tomato sauce
1½ teaspoons garlic salt
1 teaspoon basil leaves
1 teaspoon oregano leaves
1 carton (12 ounces) dry cottage cheese
  (1½ cups)
¼ cup grated Romano cheese
1 egg
1½ pounds zucchini, cut lengthwise into
  ¼-inch slices
2 tablespoons all-purpose flour
1 cup shredded mozzarella cheese
  (4 ounces)
¼ cup grated Romano cheese

Heat oven to 350°. Cook and stir meat in large skillet until brown. Drain off fat. Stir in tomato sauce, garlic salt, basil leaves and oregano leaves; heat to boiling. Reduce heat and simmer uncovered until mixture is consistency of spaghetti sauce, about 10 minutes. Coat baking pan, 9 × 9 × 2 inches, with vegetable spray-on for cookware. Mix cottage cheese, ¼ cup Romano cheese and the egg. Layer half each of zucchini, flour, cottage cheese mixture, meat sauce and mozzarella cheese; repeat. Sprinkle ¼ cup Romano cheese on top. Bake uncovered 45 minutes. Let stand 20 minutes before serving. Cut into squares.

Taco Feast

1½ pounds lean ground beef
1 envelope (1¼ ounces) taco seasoning
  mix
1 cup water
12 ready-to-serve taco shells
¾ cup shredded lettuce
¾ cup chopped tomato
¾ cup chopped green pepper
¾ cup chopped onion
¾ cup chopped cucumber
¾ cup shredded Cheddar cheese
Salsa

Heat oven to 350°. Cook and stir meat in large skillet until brown. Drain off fat. Stir in taco seasoning mix and water; heat to boiling. Reduce heat and simmer uncovered 15 to 20 minutes, stirring occasionally. While meat simmers, heat taco shells on ungreased baking sheet in oven 3 to 5 minutes.

Spoon ¼ cup meat mixture into each taco shell. Add 1 tablespoon each lettuce, tomato, green pepper, onion, cucumber and cheese. Top with salsa.

Stuffed Green Peppers

6 SERVINGS

6 large green peppers
5 cups boiling water
1½ pounds lean ground beef
2 tablespoons chopped onion
½ teaspoon salt
⅛ teaspoon garlic powder
1 cup cooked rice
1 cup tomato juice
6 thick tomato slices

Cut thin slice from stem end of each pepper; remove all seeds and membranes. Cook peppers in boiling water 5 minutes; drain.

Heat oven to 350°. Cook and stir meat and onion in large skillet until meat is brown and onion is tender. Drain off fat. Stir in salt, garlic powder, rice and tomato juice; heat to boiling.

Lightly stuff each pepper with ½ cup meat mixture. Stand peppers upright in ungreased baking dish, 11¾ × 7½ × 1¾ inches. Cover with aluminum foil and bake 45 minutes. Top each pepper with a tomato slice and sprinkle with salt. Bake uncovered 15 minutes.

Oriental Vegetable Meat Roll

6 SERVINGS

1 pound lean ground beef
1 cup soft whole wheat bread crumbs
    (about 2 slices bread)
1 egg
⅓ cup coarsely chopped green onions
    (with tops)
2 tablespoons soy sauce
1 teaspoon ground ginger
¼ teaspoon pepper
1 can (8 ounces) water chestnuts, chopped
1 jar (2.5 ounces) mushroom stems and
    pieces, drained
1 jar (2 ounces) diced pimientos, drained

Heat oven to 350°. Mix all ingredients except water chestnuts, mushrooms and pimientos. Shape mixture into a 12 × 10-inch rectangle on waxed paper. Mix remaining ingredients. Spread over beef mixture to within 1 inch of edges; press into beef mixture. Roll up, beginning at narrow end, using waxed paper to help roll. Pinch edges and ends of roll to seal. Place roll, seam side down, on rack sprayed with nonstick cooking spray in broiler pan. Bake uncovered until done, 1 to 1¼ hours. Let stand 10 minutes before slicing.

Following pages: Stuffed Green Peppers

Meatballs in Dijon Sauce

1 pound lean ground beef
1 slice whole wheat bread, crumbled
1 small finely chopped onion (about
*   ¹/₄ cup)*
1 tablespoon Dijon mustard
¹/₄ teaspoon salt
¹/₄ teaspoon pepper
Dijon Sauce (below)
3 cups hot cooked noodles

DIJON SAUCE

3 tablespoons all-purpose flour
1 tablespoon cornstarch
1¹/₂ teaspoons instant beef bouillon
1 cup water
1 cup skim milk
3 tablespoons finely snipped chives
2 tablespoons Dijon mustard
¹/₄ teaspoon pepper
1 teaspoon lemon juice

Heat oven to 400°. Mix all ingredients except Dijon Sauce and noodles; shape into twenty-four 1¹/₄-inch meatballs. Place on rack sprayed with nonstick cooking spray in broiler pan. Bake uncovered until done and light brown, 20 to 35 minutes.

Prepare Dijon Sauce; add meatballs, stirring gently, until meatballs are hot. Serve over noodles.

Mix flour, cornstarch, bouillon (dry) and water in 2-quart saucepan; stir in remaining ingredients. Cook over medium heat until mixture thickens and boils, stirring constantly. Boil and stir 1 minute.

TO MICROWAVE: Prepare meatballs as directed and place in rectangular microwavable dish, 12 × 7¹/₂ × 2 inches. Cover with waxed paper and microwave on high 3 minutes; rearrange meatballs. Cover and microwave until no longer pink inside, 4 to 6 minutes longer. Let stand covered 3 minutes; drain. Mix all ingredients for Dijon Sauce in 2-quart microwavable casserole. Microwave uncovered, stirring every minute until thickened, 4 to 6 minutes. Stir in meatballs; serve over noodles.

Beef and Bulgur Casserole

8 SERVINGS

1½ pounds lean ground beef
1 large onion, chopped (about 1 cup)
1 cup uncooked bulgur
2 cups chopped tomatoes (about
*   2 medium)*
2 cups water
3 tablespoons snipped parsley
2 teaspoons instant beef bouillon
1½ teaspoons salt
1 teaspoon snipped fresh oregano leaves
*   or ½ teaspoon dried oregano leaves*
¼ teaspoon instant minced garlic
¼ teaspoon pepper
½ cup grated Parmesan cheese

Heat oven to 350°. Cook and stir ground beef and onion in 10-inch nonstick skillet until beef is brown; drain. Stir in remaining ingredients except cheese. Pour into ungreased 2-quart casserole or rectangular dish, 12 × 7½ × 2 inches. Cover and bake until bulgur is tender, about 45 minutes. Stir in cheese. Sprinkle with snipped parsley, if desired.

TO MICROWAVE: Crumble ground beef into 3-quart microwavable casserole; add onion. Cover with waxed paper and microwave on high 5 minutes; break up and stir. Cover and microwave until very little pink remains, 4 to 6 minutes longer; drain. Stir in remaining ingredients except cheese. Cover and microwave 10 minutes; stir. Cover and microwave until bulgur is tender, 10 to 14 minutes longer. Stir in cheese. Sprinkle with snipped parsley, if desired.

Turkey Burgers

4 SERVINGS

1 pound ground turkey
1 teaspoon salt
¼ teaspoon sage
2 tablespoons finely chopped onion
¼ cup jellied cranberry sauce
¼ teaspoon horseradish
¼ cup water

Coat large skillet with vegetable spray-on for cookware. Mix meat, salt, sage and onion. Shape mixture into 4 patties, about 3½ inches in diameter and ¾ inch thick. Cook in skillet over medium heat, turning frequently, until light brown and done, about 15 minutes.

While patties cook, heat remaining ingredients until hot, stirring occasionally. Spoon 2 tablespoons cranberry mixture onto each patty.

Turkey Taco Salad

3 flour tortillas (8 inches in diameter)
1/2 pound ground turkey
1/3 cup water
1 to 2 teaspoons chili powder
1/2 teaspoon salt
1/4 teaspoon garlic powder
1/4 teaspoon ground red pepper
1 can (8 ounces) kidney beans, drained
5 cups shredded lettuce
1 cup chopped tomato (about 1 medium)
1/2 cup shredded Monterey Jack cheese
(2 ounces)
1 small onion, chopped (about 1/4 cup)
1/4 cup reduced-calorie Thousand Island
dressing
1/4 cup reduced-calorie sour cream
4 pitted ripe olives, sliced

Heat oven to 400°. Cut tortillas into 12 wedges, or strips about 3 × 1/4 inch. Place in ungreased jelly roll pan, 15½ × 10½ × 1 inch. Bake, stirring at least once, until golden brown and crisp, 6 to 8 minutes; cool.

Cook and stir ground turkey in 10-inch non-stick skillet over medium heat until brown. Stir in water, chili powder, salt, garlic powder, red pepper and kidney beans. Heat to boiling; reduce heat. Simmer uncovered, stirring occasionally, until liquid is absorbed, 2 to 3 minutes; cool 10 minutes.

Mix lettuce, tomato, cheese and onion in large bowl; toss with Thousand Island dressing. Divide among 4 serving plates; top each salad with about ½ cup turkey mixture. Arrange tortilla wedges around salad. Garnish with sour cream and ripe olives.

Chili-stuffed Peppers

3 large bell peppers (green, red or yellow)
1/2 pound ground turkey, cooked and
drained
1 cup cooked rice
1/4 cup chopped onion (about 1 small)
1 teaspoon ground cumin
1/2 teaspoon salt
1/4 teaspoon pepper
2 eggs
2 cloves garlic, finely chopped
1 can (4 ounces) chopped green chilies
1 jar (2 ounces) diced pimientos, drained
1/2 cup shredded Monterey Jack cheese

Heat oven to 350°. Cut bell peppers lengthwise into halves. Remove seeds and membranes; rinse peppers. Cook 2 minutes in enough boiling water to cover; drain. Mix remaining ingredients except cheese; loosely stuff each pepper half. Arrange peppers in rectangular baking dish, 12 × 7½ × 2 inches, sprayed with nonstick cooking spray. Cover and bake until rice mixture is hot, about 30 minutes. Uncover; sprinkle with cheese. Bake until cheese is melted, about 5 minutes longer.

Turkey Meatballs Mandarin

1 pound ground turkey
1 teaspoon salt
1 teaspoon instant minced onion
1/4 teaspoon garlic powder
1 tablespoon chopped pimiento
1 tablespoon soy sauce
1 egg
4 cups water
1 teaspoon salt
2 tablespoons soy sauce
1/2 teaspoon crushed gingerroot or
   1/4 teaspoon ground ginger
1 package (6 ounces) frozen Chinese pea
   pods
1 teaspoon cornstarch
1 tablespoon water
3 cups hot cooked rice
Parsley
1 can (11 ounces) mandarin orange
   segments, drained

Mix meat, 1 teaspoon salt, the onion, garlic powder, pimiento, 1 tablespoon soy sauce and the egg thoroughly. Shape mixture into 1½-inch balls.

In large skillet, heat 4 cups water, 1 teaspoon salt, 2 tablespoons soy sauce and the gingerroot to boiling. Place meatballs in seasoned water; heat to boiling. Reduce heat; cover and simmer until meatballs are done, about 30 minutes. While meatballs simmer, cook pea pods as directed on package; drain.

With slotted spoon, remove meatballs to warm platter. Strain liquid; reserve 1 cup. Mix cornstarch and 1 tablespoon water in same skillet. Stir in reserved liquid. Cook, stirring constantly, until mixture thickens and boils. Boil and stir 1 minute.

Arrange meatballs on rice. Arrange pea pods around meatballs; garnish with parsley and orange segments. Serve with gravy.

BEEF MEATBALLS MANDARIN: Substitute 1 pound lean ground beef for the ground turkey; decrease salt in meat mixture to ¾ teaspoon.

Following pages: Turkey Taco Salad

LOW-CALORIE DINNERS   *49*

Ginger Pork on Pineapple

1 pineapple
1 pound lean ground pork
1 small onion, chopped (about ¼ cup)
1 tablespoon packed brown sugar
1 tablespoon vinegar
1 teaspoon ground ginger
½ teaspoon salt
¼ teaspoon pepper
1 medium green bell pepper, cut into
  1-inch pieces
1 can (8 ounces) tomato sauce
1 can (8 ounces) sliced water chestnuts,
  drained

Pare pineapple; cut crosswise into 6 slices. Place pineapple on rack sprayed with nonstick cooking spray in broiler pan.

Cook and stir ground pork and onion in 10-inch nonstick skillet over medium heat until pork is light brown; drain. Stir in remaining ingredients. Heat to boiling; reduce heat. Simmer uncovered, stirring occasionally, until bell pepper is crisp-tender, about 10 minutes.

Set oven control to broil. Broil pineapple with tops 4 to 5 inches from heat 5 minutes; turn. Broil until hot and bubbly, 3 to 5 minutes longer. Serve pork mixture over pineapple.

Italian Sausage and Vegetables

1 spaghetti squash (about 3 pounds)
1 pound Italian sausage, casing removed
  and crumbled, or bulk Italian sausage
1 medium onion, chopped (about ½ cup)
1 cup coarsely chopped zucchini (about
  1 medium)
¼ cup snipped parsley
1 large clove garlic, crushed
1 tablespoon dried basil leaves
3 cups coarsely chopped tomatoes (about
  4 medium)
⅓ cup grated Parmesan cheese
½ teaspoon salt
¼ teaspoon pepper

Heat oven to 400°. Prick squash with fork. Bake until tender, about 1 hour. Cook and stir sausage and onion in 10-inch nonstick skillet over medium heat until sausage is done, about 10 minutes; drain. Stir in zucchini, parsley, garlic and basil. Cover and cook 3 minutes. Stir in tomatoes and cheese. Cut squash into halves; remove seeds and fibers. Remove spaghettilike strands with 2 forks; toss with salt and pepper. Serve sausage mixture over squash.

Lamb Patties with Fresh Mint Sauce

4 SERVINGS,
WITH 1½ TABLESPOONS SAUCE EACH

Fresh Mint Sauce (below)
1 pound lean ground lamb
⅔ cup soft bread crumbs
⅓ cup dry red wine
½ teaspoon salt
*¼ teaspoon dried rosemary leaves,
   crushed*
2 small cloves garlic, finely chopped

FRESH MINT SAUCE

*¼ cup mashed pared kiwifruit (about
   1 medium)*
*1 tablespoon snipped fresh mint leaves or
   ½ teaspoon dried mint leaves, crushed*
2 teaspoons sugar
2 teaspoons lime juice

Prepare Fresh Mint Sauce. Set oven control to broil. Mix remaining ingredients. Shape lamb mixture into 4 patties, each about 1 inch thick. Place patties on rack sprayed with nonstick cooking spray in broiler pan. Broil with tops about 3 inches from heat, 5 to 7 minutes on each side for medium, to desired doneness. Serve with Fresh Mint Sauce. Garnish with mint leaves and sliced kiwifruit, if desired.

Mix all ingredients.

TO MICROWAVE: Prepare Fresh Mint Sauce and lamb patties. Place patties on microwavable rack in microwavable dish. Cover with vented plastic wrap and microwave on high 3 minutes; rotate dish ½ turn. Microwave until patties are almost done, 3 to 4 minutes longer. Let stand covered 3 minutes. Serve with Fresh Mint Sauce. Garnish with mint leaves and sliced kiwifruit, if desired.

Following pages: Italian Sausage and Vegetables

· 4 ·

CASEROLES

One-Skillet Spaghetti

7 SERVINGS

1 pound ground beef
2 medium onions, chopped (about 1 cup)
1 can (29 ounces) tomatoes
3/4 cup chopped green pepper
1/2 cup water
1 can (4 ounces) mushroom stems and
   pieces, drained
2 teaspoons salt
1 teaspoon sugar
1 teaspoon chili powder
1 package (7 ounces) uncooked thin
   spaghetti, broken into pieces
1 cup shredded Cheddar cheese (4 ounces)

Cook and stir meat and onions in large skillet or Dutch oven until meat is brown. Drain off fat. Stir in tomatoes (with liquid) and remaining ingredients except Cheddar cheese; break up tomatoes.

TO COOK IN SKILLET: Heat mixture to boiling. Reduce heat; cover and simmer, stirring occasionally, until spaghetti is tender, about 30 minutes. (A small amount of water can be added if necessary.) Sprinkle with cheese. Cover and heat until cheese is melted.

TO COOK IN OVEN: Pour mixture into ungreased 2- or 2½-quart casserole. Cover and bake in 375° oven, stirring occasionally, until spaghetti is tender, about 45 minutes. Uncover; sprinkle with shredded Cheddar cheese and bake about 5 minutes.

Double-Cheese Hamburger Casserole
5 SERVINGS

4 ounces uncooked egg noodles (about
  2 cups)
1 pound ground beef
1/3 cup chopped onion
1/4 cup chopped celery
1 can (8 ounces) tomato sauce
1 teaspoon salt
1 package (3 ounces) cream cheese,
  softened
1/2 cup creamed cottage cheese
1/4 cup dairy sour cream
1 medium tomato, if desired

Cook noodles as directed on package; drain. While noodles are cooking, cook and stir meat, onion and celery in large skillet until meat is brown. Drain off fat. Stir in noodles, tomato sauce, salt, cream cheese, cottage cheese and sour cream.

TO COOK IN SKILLET: Heat mixture to boiling. Reduce heat and simmer uncovered 5 minutes, stirring frequently. Remove from heat. Cut tomato into thin slices and arrange on meat mixture. Cover until tomato slices are warm, about 5 minutes.

TO COOK IN OVEN: Turn mixture into ungreased 1½-quart casserole. Cut tomato into thin slices and arrange on meat mixture. Cover and bake in 350° oven until hot, about 30 minutes.

Spaghetti and Beef Sauce
6 SERVINGS

1 pound ground beef
1 large onion, chopped (about 1 cup)
1 clove garlic, crushed
1 teaspoon sugar
1 teaspoon dried oregano leaves
3/4 teaspoon salt
3/4 teaspoon dried basil leaves
1/2 teaspoon dried marjoram leaves
1 can (16 ounces) whole tomatoes,
  undrained
1 can (8 ounces) tomato sauce
4 cups hot cooked spaghetti

Cook and stir ground beef, the onion and garlic in 10-inch skillet until beef is light brown; drain. Stir in remaining ingredients except spaghetti; break up tomatoes. Heat to boiling; reduce heat. Cover and simmer, stirring occasionally, 1 hour. Serve over spaghetti and, if desired, with grated Parmesan cheese.

Lasagne

MEAT SAUCE

1 pound ground beef
2 cloves garlic, minced
*3 cans (8 ounces each) tomato sauce**
½ teaspoon salt
¼ teaspoon pepper
½ teaspoon oregano leaves

Cook and stir meat and garlic in large skillet until meat is brown. Drain off fat. Stir in tomato sauce, salt, pepper and oregano leaves. Cover and simmer 20 minutes.

While Meat Sauce is simmering, cook noodles as directed on package; drain.

*You can substitute 1 can (16 ounces) tomatoes and 1 can (6 ounces) tomato paste for the tomato sauce.

NOODLES AND CHEESE

1 package (8 ounces) uncooked lasagne noodles
1 carton (12 ounces) creamed cottage cheese (1½ cups)
2 cups shredded mozzarella or Swiss cheese (8 ounces)
⅓ cup grated Parmesan cheese

Heat oven to 350°. In ungreased baking pan, 13 × 9 × 2 inches, or baking dish, 11¾ × 7½ × 1¾ inches, layer half each of the noodles, meat sauce, cottage cheese and mozzarella cheese; repeat. Sprinkle Parmesan cheese over top. Bake uncovered until hot and bubbly, about 40 minutes.

All-American Hot Dish

1 pound ground beef
1 medium onion, chopped (about ½ cup)
1 can (8 ounces) whole kernel corn, undrained
1 can (8 ounces) tomato sauce
¼ cup halved pitted ripe olives
4 ounces uncooked noodles (about 2 cups)
2 cups water
1 teaspoon oregano leaves
½ teaspoon salt
¼ teaspoon pepper
1 cup shredded Cheddar cheese (4 ounces)

Cook and stir meat and onion in large skillet until meat is brown. Drain off fat. Stir in corn (with liquid) and remaining ingredients.

TO COOK IN SKILLET: Heat mixture to boiling. Reduce heat and simmer uncovered, stirring occasionally, until noodles are tender, about 20 minutes.

TO COOK IN OVEN: Pour mixture into ungreased 2-quart casserole. Cover and bake in 375° oven 30 minutes, stirring occasionally. Uncover and bake until mixture thickens, about 15 minutes.

Manicotti

MEAT FILLING

1 pound ground beef
1/4 cup chopped onion (about 1 small)
3 slices bread, torn into small pieces
1 1/2 cups shredded mozzarella cheese
1 egg
1/2 cup milk
1 tablespoon snipped parsley
1/4 teaspoon pepper

PASTA

1 package (8 ounces) uncooked manicotti
   shells

TOMATO SAUCE

1 can (4 ounces) mushroom stems and
   pieces, undrained
1 can (15 ounces) tomato sauce
1 can (12 ounces) tomato paste
1/4 cup chopped onion (about 1 small)
1 clove garlic, minced
4 cups water
1 tablespoon Italian seasoning
1/2 teaspoon sugar
1/2 teaspoon salt
1/8 teaspoon pepper
1/3 cup grated Parmesan cheese

Cook and stir meat and 1/4 cup onion in large skillet until meat is brown. Drain off fat. Remove from heat; stir in remaining ingredients for Meat Filling.

Fill uncooked manicotti shells, packing the filling into both ends. Place shells in ungreased baking pan, 13 × 9 × 2 inches.

Heat oven to 375°. Heat mushrooms (with liquid) and the remaining ingredients for Tomato Sauce except cheese to boiling, stirring occasionally. Reduce heat and simmer uncovered 5 minutes. Pour sauce over shells. Cover with aluminum foil and bake until shells are tender, 1 1/2 to 1 3/4 hours. Sprinkle with cheese. Cool 5 to 10 minutes before serving.

Following pages: Manicotti

Hearty Beef Supper

7 SERVINGS

2 pounds ground beef
1 large onion, chopped (about 1 cup)
1 cup uncooked bulgur
2 cups chopped tomato (about 2 medium)
2 cups water
3 tablespoons snipped parsley
2 teaspoons instant beef bouillon
1 teaspoon salt
½ teaspoon oregano leaves
¼ teaspoon instant minced garlic
¼ teaspoon pepper
¼ cup grated Parmesan cheese

Cook and stir meat and onion in large skillet until meat is brown. Drain off fat. Stir in remaining ingredients except cheese; heat to boiling. Reduce heat; cover and simmer, stirring occasionally, until wheat is tender, about 30 minutes. (A small amount of water can be added if necessary.) Stir in cheese. Garnish with additional snipped parsley and Parmesan cheese.

Mexican Spoon Bread Casserole

6 TO 8 SERVINGS

MEAT MIXTURE

1½ pounds ground beef
1 large onion, chopped (about 1 cup)
¼ cup chopped green pepper, if desired
1 clove garlic, minced
1 can (15 ounces) tomato sauce
1 can (11 ounces) whole kernel corn
1½ teaspoons salt
2 to 3 teaspoons chili powder
⅛ teaspoon pepper
½ cup sliced ripe olives

CORNMEAL TOPPING

1½ cups milk
½ cup yellow cornmeal
½ teaspoon salt
¾ cup shredded Cheddar cheese
2 eggs, beaten

Heat oven to 375°. Cook and stir meat, onion, green pepper and garlic in large skillet until onion is tender. Drain off fat. Stir in tomato sauce, corn (with liquid), 1½ teaspoons salt, the chili powder, pepper and olives; heat to boiling. Reduce heat and simmer uncovered while preparing Cornmeal Topping.

Mix milk, cornmeal and ½ teaspoon salt in saucepan. Cook and stir over medium heat just until mixture boils. Remove from heat; stir in cheese and eggs.

Turn hot Meat Mixture into ungreased 2½- to 3-quart casserole. Immediately pour topping onto Meat Mixture. Bake uncovered until knife inserted in topping comes out clean, about 40 minutes.

Spanish Rice with Beef

6 SERVINGS

1 pound ground beef
1 medium onion, chopped (about ½ cup)
1 cup uncooked regular rice
⅔ cup chopped green pepper
1 can (16 ounces) stewed tomatoes
5 slices bacon, crisply cooked and
    crumbled
2 cups water
1 teaspoon chili powder
½ teaspoon oregano leaves
¾ teaspoon salt
⅛ teaspoon pepper

Cook and stir meat and onion in large skillet until meat is brown. Drain off fat. Stir in remaining ingredients.

TO COOK IN SKILLET: Heat mixture to boiling. Reduce heat; cover and simmer, stirring occasionally, until rice is tender, about 30 minutes. (A small amount of water can be added if necessary.)

TO COOK IN OVEN: Pour mixture into ungreased 2-quart casserole. Cover and bake in 375° oven, stirring occasionally, until rice is tender, about 45 minutes.

Mexican Fiesta Casserole

5 OR 6 SERVINGS

1 pound ground beef
Salt and pepper
1 cup shredded Cheddar cheese (4 ounces)
1 cup dairy sour cream
⅔ cup mayonnaise or salad dressing
2 tablespoons finely chopped onion
2 cups variety baking mix
½ cup water
2 to 3 medium tomatoes, thinly sliced
¾ cup chopped green pepper

Heat oven to 375°. Cook and stir meat in skillet until brown. Drain off fat. Season meat with salt and pepper; set aside. Mix cheese, sour cream, mayonnaise and onion; set aside.

Stir baking mix and water until a soft dough forms. With floured fingers, pat dough in greased baking pan, 13 × 9 × 2 inches, pressing dough ½ inch up sides of pan. Layer meat, tomato slices and green pepper on dough. Spoon sour cream mixture over top and sprinkle with paprika, if desired. Bake uncovered until edges of dough are light brown, 25 to 30 minutes. Cool 5 minutes, then cut into squares.

Following pages: Mexican Spoon Bread Casserole

Green Lasagne with Two Sauces

Meat Sauce (below)
Cheese Filling (below)
Creamy Sauce (right)
12 spinach lasagne noodles, cooked and
   drained

Heat oven to 350°. Prepare Meat Sauce, Cheese Filling and Creamy Sauce. Reserve ½ cup of the Cheese Filling. Spread 1 cup of the Meat Sauce in ungreased oblong baking dish, 13½ × 9 × 2 inches. Layer 3 lasagne noodles, ½ of the Creamy Sauce, ½ of the remaining Cheese Filling, 3 lasagne noodles and ½ of the remaining Meat Sauce; repeat. Sprinkle with reserved Cheese Filling. Cook uncovered in oven until hot and bubbly, about 35 minutes. Let stand 10 minutes before cutting.

MEAT SAUCE

8 ounces bulk Italian sausage, crumbled
4 ounces smoked sliced chicken or turkey,
   finely chopped
1 large onion, finely chopped (about
   1 cup)
1 medium stalk celery, finely chopped
1 medium carrot, finely shredded
2 cloves garlic, finely chopped
1¾ cups water
¾ cup dry red wine
⅓ cup tomato paste
½ teaspoon Italian herb seasoning
⅛ teaspoon pepper
Dash of ground nutmeg

Cook and stir sausage until light brown; drain. Stir in remaining ingredients. Heat to boiling; reduce heat. Simmer uncovered, stirring occasionally, 1 hour.

CHEESE FILLING

2 cups shredded mozzarella cheese
1½ cups grated Parmesan cheese
¼ cup snipped parsley

Toss cheeses and parsley.

CREAMY SAUCE

1/3 cup margarine or butter
1/3 cup all-purpose flour
1 teaspoon salt
Dash of ground nutmeg
3 cups milk

Heat margarine over low heat until melted. Blend in flour, salt and nutmeg. Cook over low heat, stirring constantly, until smooth and bubbly; remove from heat. Stir in milk. Heat to boiling, stirring constantly. Boil and stir 1 minute; cover and keep warm. (If sauce thickens, beat in small amount of milk. Sauce should be the consistency of heavy cream.)

Hungry Boy's Casserole

6 SERVINGS

1 pound ground beef
2 stalks celery, sliced (about 1 cup)
1 medium onion, chopped (about 1/2 cup)
1 clove garlic, minced
1 can (16 ounces) whole kernel corn
1 can (16 ounces) pork and beans
1/2 cup chopped green pepper
1 teaspoon salt
1 can (6 ounces) tomato paste

Cook and stir meat, celery, onion and garlic in large skillet until meat is brown. Drain off fat. Stir in corn (with liquid) and remaining ingredients.

TO COOK IN SKILLET: Heat mixture to boiling. Reduce heat; cover and simmer 10 minutes, stirring occasionally.

TO COOK IN OVEN: Pour mixture into ungreased 2-quart casserole. Cover and bake in 375° oven until hot and bubbly, about 45 minutes.

Skillet Beef and Noodles

4 TO 5 SERVINGS

1 pound ground beef
1 envelope (about 1 1/2 ounces) onion soup mix
1 can (1 pound 12 ounces) tomatoes
4 ounces uncooked noodles (about 2 cups)

In large skillet, cook and stir ground beef until brown. Stir in remaining ingredients; heat to boiling. Reduce heat; cover and simmer until noodles are tender, about 20 minutes, stirring occasionally.

Baked Macaroni with Beef and Cheese

6 SERVINGS

7 ounces uncooked ziti or elbow macaroni
(about 2 cups)
3/4 pound ground beef
1 small onion, chopped (about 1/4 cup)
1 can (15 ounces) tomato sauce
1 teaspoon salt
1 1/2 cups grated Parmesan or Romano
cheese (6 ounces)
1/8 teaspoon ground cinnamon
1 1/4 cups milk
3 tablespoons margarine or butter
2 eggs, beaten
1/8 teaspoon ground nutmeg

Heat oven to 325°. Cook macaroni as directed on package; drain. Cook and stir beef and onion in 10-inch skillet until beef is light brown; drain. Stir in tomato sauce and salt. Spread half the macaroni in greased square baking dish, 8 × 8 × 2 inches; cover with beef mixture. Mix 1/2 cup of the cheese and the cinnamon; sprinkle over beef mixture. Cover with remaining macaroni.

Cook and stir milk and margarine in 2-quart saucepan until margarine is melted. Remove from heat. Stir at least half the milk mixture gradually into beaten eggs. Blend into milk mixture in saucepan; pour over macaroni. Sprinkle with remaining 1 cup cheese. Cook uncovered in oven until brown and center is set, about 50 minutes. Sprinkle with nutmeg. Garnish with parsley, if desired.

Moussaka

8 SERVINGS

1 large eggplant (about 2 pounds)
2 tablespoons margarine or butter
1 1/2 pounds ground lamb or beef
1 medium onion, chopped (about 1/2 cup)
1 can (15 ounces) tomato sauce
3/4 cup red wine or beef broth
1 tablespoon snipped parsley
2 teaspoons salt
1/4 teaspoon pepper
1/4 teaspoon ground nutmeg
White Sauce (right)
1 cup grated Parmesan cheese
2/3 cup dry bread crumbs
1 egg, beaten
Tomato Sauce (right)

Heat oven to 375°. Cut eggplant crosswise into 1/2-inch slices. Cook slices in small amount boiling, salted water (1/2 teaspoon salt to 1 cup water) until tender, 5 to 8 minutes. Drain. Heat margarine in 12-inch skillet until melted. Cook and stir lamb and onion until lamb is light brown; drain. Stir in tomato sauce, wine, parsley, salt, pepper and nutmeg. Cook uncovered over medium heat until half the liquid is absorbed, about 20 minutes. Prepare White Sauce.

Stir 2/3 cup of the cheese, 1/3 cup of the bread crumbs and the egg into meat mixture; remove from heat. Sprinkle remaining bread crumbs evenly in greased oblong baking dish, 13 1/2 × 9 × 2 inches. Arrange half the eggplant slices in baking dish; cover with meat mixture. Sprinkle 2 tablespoons of the remaining cheese over meat mixture; top with remaining eggplant slices. Pour White Sauce over mixture; sprinkle with remaining cheese. Cook uncovered in oven 45 minutes. Prepare Tomato Sauce. Let moussaka stand 20 minutes before serving. Cut into squares; serve with Tomato Sauce.

WHITE SAUCE

1/4 cup margarine or butter
1/4 cup all-purpose flour
3/4 teaspoon salt
1/4 teaspoon ground nutmeg
2 cups milk
2 eggs, slightly beaten

Heat margarine over low heat until melted. Blend in flour, salt and nutmeg. Cook over low heat, stirring constantly, until smooth and bubbly; remove from heat. Stir in milk. Heat to boiling, stirring constantly. Boil and stir 1 minute. Gradually stir at least one-fourth of the hot mixture into eggs. Blend back into hot mixture in pan.

TOMATO SAUCE

1 medium onion, finely chopped (about
   1/2 cup)
1 clove garlic, finely chopped
1 tablespoon olive or vegetable oil
2 cups chopped ripe tomatoes
1/2 cup water
1 1/2 teaspoons salt
1 teaspoon dried basil leaves
1/2 teaspoon sugar
1/4 teaspoon pepper
1 bay leaf, crushed
1 can (6 ounces) tomato paste

Cook and stir onion and garlic in oil in 3-quart saucepan over medium heat until onion is tender. Add remaining ingredients except tomato paste. Heat to boiling, stirring constantly; reduce heat. Simmer uncovered until thickened, about 30 minutes. Stir in tomato paste. (Add 2 to 3 tablespoons water, if necessary, for desired consistency.)

Following pages: Moussaka

Ground Lamb and Eggplant

1 medium eggplant (1½ to 2 pounds)
½ teaspoon salt
½ cup all-purpose flour
Vegetable oil
1 pound ground lamb
1 medium onion, chopped (about ½ cup)
2 tablespoons margarine or butter
1 can (8 ounces) tomato sauce
1 cup dry red wine
2 tablespoons snipped parsley
¼ teaspoon pepper
¼ teaspoon ground nutmeg
1 egg, beaten
½ cup grated Parmesan or Romano cheese
¼ cup dry bread crumbs
3 tablespoons margarine or butter
3 tablespoons all-purpose flour
½ teaspoon salt
¼ teaspoon ground nutmeg
1¾ cups milk
2 eggs, slightly beaten
¼ cup grated Parmesan or Romano cheese
¼ cup dry bread crumbs
4 tablespoons grated Parmesan or Romano cheese

Pare eggplant; cut crosswise into ¼-inch slices. Sprinkle slices with ½ teaspoon salt. Coat with ½ cup flour; shake off excess. Heat 2 tablespoons oil in 10-inch skillet. Cook several eggplant slices in hot oil until golden brown on both sides. Repeat with remaining slices, adding more oil when necessary; drain.

Cook and stir ground lamb and onion in 2 tablespoons margarine in 10-inch skillet until lamb is brown. Stir in tomato sauce, wine, parsley, pepper and ¼ teaspoon nutmeg. Cook uncovered until half of liquid is absorbed, about 20 minutes. Stir in 1 beaten egg, ½ cup cheese and ¼ cup dry bread crumbs. Remove from heat.

Heat oven to 375°. Heat 3 tablespoons margarine in 2-quart saucepan until melted. Stir in 3 tablespoons flour, ½ teaspoon salt and ¼ teaspoon nutmeg. Cook over low heat, stirring constantly, until mixture is smooth and bubbly. Stir in milk. Heat to boiling, stirring constantly. Stir small amount of hot milk mixture into 2 slightly beaten eggs. Stir egg mixture into hot mixture in saucepan. Stir in ¼ cup cheese.

Grease rectangular baking dish, 12 × 7½ × 2 inches, or square pan, 9 × 9 × 2 inches. Sprinkle ¼ cup dry bread crumbs evenly in dish. Arrange half of the eggplant slices in dish; cover with lamb mixture. Sprinkle with 2 tablespoons of the cheese; top with remaining eggplant slices. Pour sauce over eggplant slices; sprinkle with remaining 2 tablespoons cheese. Bake uncovered until golden brown and bubbly, about 45 minutes. Remove from oven; let stand 20 minutes before serving.

· 5 ·

SUPER SUPPERS

Latin Meatballs

2 jalapeño peppers
1 pound ground beef
1 egg
1/2 cup dry bread crumbs
1/4 cup milk
1/4 cup shredded Monterey Jack cheese
1 small onion, finely chopped (about
   1/4 cup)
1 teaspoon salt
1/4 teaspoon pepper
Salsa (below)

Heat oven to 400°. Remove stems, seeds and membranes from peppers; chop peppers. Mix peppers, beef, egg, bread crumbs, milk, cheese, onion, salt and pepper. Shape mixture into 1-inch balls. Place in ungreased pan, 13 × 9 × 2 inches. Cook uncovered in oven until brown, 15 to 20 minutes. Serve with Salsa.

SALSA

1 can (8 ounces) tomato sauce
1 medium tomato, chopped
2 cloves garlic, finely chopped
2 tablespoons snipped parsley
1 tablespoon vinegar
1/8 teaspoon ground cumin
1/8 teaspoon salt

Heat all ingredients.

Following pages: Latin Meatballs, left, and Swedish Meatballs, right (page 76)

Swedish Meatballs

6 TO 8 SERVINGS

1 pound ground beef
½ pound ground pork
¾ cup dry bread crumbs
¼ cup milk
1 egg
1 small onion, finely chopped (about
    ¼ cup)
1½ teaspoons salt
¼ teaspoon ground nutmeg
¼ teaspoon pepper
3 tablespoons all-purpose flour
¾ cup water
1 cup half-and-half
1 teaspoon instant beef bouillon
½ teaspoon salt
Snipped parsley

Heat oven to 350°. Mix beef, pork, bread crumbs, milk, egg, onion, 1½ teaspoons salt, the nutmeg and pepper. Shape mixture into 1-inch balls. (For easy shaping, dip hands into cold water from time to time.) Place meatballs on ungreased jelly roll pan, 15½ × 10½ × 1 inch, or in 2 oblong pans, 13 × 9 × 2 inches. Cook uncovered in oven until light brown, about 20 minutes.

Remove meatballs to serving dish; keep warm. Place 3 tablespoons pan drippings in sauce-pan; stir in flour. Cook over low heat, stirring constantly, until mixture is smooth and bubbly. Remove from heat. Stir in water, half-and-half, bouillon (dry) and ½ teaspoon salt. Heat to boiling, stirring constantly. Boil and stir 1 minute. Pour gravy over meatballs; sprinkle with parsley.

Meat Loaf

6 SERVINGS

1½ pounds ground beef
½ cup dry bread crumbs, ½ cup wheat
    germ or ¾ cup quick-cooking oats
1 egg
1 cup milk
1 small onion, chopped (about ¼ cup)
1 tablespoon Worcestershire sauce
½ teaspoon salt
½ teaspoon dry mustard
¼ teaspoon pepper
¼ teaspoon sage
⅛ teaspoon garlic powder
½ cup ketchup, chili sauce or barbecue
    sauce, if desired

Heat oven to 350°. Mix all ingredients except ketchup. Spread mixture in ungreased loaf pan, 9 × 5 × 3 inches, or shape into loaf in ungreased baking pan. Spoon ketchup onto loaf. Bake uncovered 1 to 1¼ hours.

Cheese-topped Pie

1 pound ground beef
1 small green pepper, chopped (about ½ cup)
1 small onion, chopped (about ¼ cup)
1 jar (2 ounces) diced pimiento, drained
½ cup all-purpose flour
½ cup milk
2 egg yolks
1 egg
1 teaspoon salt
⅛ teaspoon pepper
1 tablespoon margarine or butter
1 tablespoon all-purpose flour
½ teaspoon dry mustard
¼ teaspoon salt
Dash of cayenne pepper
½ cup milk
1 cup shredded Cheddar cheese (about 4 ounces)
2 egg whites

Cook and stir ground beef, green pepper and onion until beef is brown; drain. Stir in pimiento. Spread beef mixture in ungreased pie plate, 9 × 1¼ inches. Beat ½ cup flour, ½ cup milk, the egg yolks, egg, 1 teaspoon salt and the pepper with hand beater until smooth. Pour over beef mixture in pie plate.

Heat oven to 375°. Heat margarine in 1-quart saucepan until melted. Blend in 1 tablespoon flour, the mustard, ¼ teaspoon salt and the cayenne pepper. Cook over low heat, stirring constantly, until smooth and bubbly; remove from heat. Stir in ½ cup milk. Heat to boiling, stirring constantly. Boil and stir 1 minute. Add cheese; cook and stir over low heat just until cheese is melted. Beat egg whites in 1½-quart bowl until stiff but not dry. Fold cheese mixture into egg whites; spread over beef mixture. Cook uncovered in oven until golden brown and knife inserted halfway between center and edge comes out clean, 20 to 25 minutes. Serve immediately.

Stuffed Cabbage Rolls

1 large head cabbage (about 2 pounds)
1½ pounds ground beef
⅓ cup uncooked regular rice
½ cup milk
1 medium onion, chopped (about ½ cup)
1 egg
2 teaspoons salt
¼ teaspoon pepper
¼ teaspoon ground allspice
½ cup water
½ cup half-and-half
1 tablespoon all-purpose flour
½ teaspoon instant beef bouillon

Remove core from cabbage. Cover cabbage with cold water; let stand about 10 minutes. Remove 12 cabbage leaves. Cover leaves with boiling water. Cover and let stand until leaves are limp, about 10 minutes; drain.

Heat oven to 350°. Mix beef, rice, milk, onion, egg, salt, pepper and allspice. Place about ⅓ cup beef mixture at stem end of each leaf. Roll leaf around beef mixture, tucking in sides. Place cabbage rolls, seam sides down, in ungreased oblong baking dish, 13½ × 9 × 2 inches. Pour water over rolls.

Cover and cook in oven until beef is done, about 1 hour. Remove cabbage rolls with slotted spoon; keep warm. Drain liquid from baking dish, reserving ½ cup liquid; skim fat.

Gradually stir half-and-half into flour in saucepan until smooth. Stir in reserved liquid and the bouillon (dry). Heat to boiling, stirring constantly. Boil and stir 1 minute. Serve sauce with cabbage rolls.

Mostaccioli with Beef and Prosciutto Sauce

8 SERVINGS

1 pound ground beef
2 medium onions, sliced
2 cloves garlic, finely chopped
¾ cup dry red wine
2 teaspoons snipped fresh rosemary leaves
    or ½ teaspoon dried rosemary leaves,
    crushed
1 teaspoon sugar
¼ teaspoon ground nutmeg
¼ teaspoon pepper
1 can (28 ounces) whole tomatoes,
    undrained
¼ pound prosciutto or dried beef, cut into
    thin strips
1 pound uncooked mostaccioli or ziti
Grated Parmesan cheese

Cook and stir ground beef, onions and garlic in 10-inch skillet until beef is brown; drain. Stir in remaining ingredients except mostaccioli and cheese; break up tomatoes. Cover and simmer 15 minutes, stirring occasionally.

Uncover and simmer about 1 hour longer, stirring occasionally. Prepare mostaccioli as directed on package; drain. Serve beef mixture over mostaccioli; sprinkle with cheese.

Baked Stuffed Papayas

4 SERVINGS

1 pound ground beef
1 medium onion, chopped (about ½ cup)
1 clove garlic, finely chopped
1 can (16 ounces) whole tomatoes,
    drained
1 jalapeño pepper, finely chopped
½ teaspoon salt
¼ teaspoon pepper
4 papayas (about 12 ounces each)
2 tablespoons grated Parmesan cheese

Heat oven to 350°. Cook and stir beef, onion and garlic in 10-inch skillet over medium heat until beef is light brown; drain. Stir in tomatoes, jalapeño pepper, salt and pepper; break up tomatoes with fork. Heat to boiling; reduce heat. Simmer uncovered until most of the liquid is evaporated, about 10 minutes.

Cut papayas lengthwise into halves; remove seeds. Place about ⅓ cup beef mixture in each papaya half; sprinkle with cheese. Arrange in shallow roasting pan. Pour very hot water into pan to within 1 inch of tops of papaya halves. Cook uncovered in oven until papayas are very tender and hot, about 30 minutes.

Following pages: Baked Stuffed Papayas

Chili

1 cup finely chopped onion
1 cup finely chopped green pepper
2 cloves garlic, finely chopped
1 cup dry red wine
1/4 cup Worcestershire sauce
2 pounds ground beef
1 tablespoon chili powder
1 teaspoon celery seed
1 teaspoon ground pepper
1/2 teaspoon salt
1/2 teaspoon ground cumin
2 cans (16 ounces each) peeled tomatoes
3 cans (15 1/2 ounces each) kidney beans, undrained

Cook and stir onion, green pepper and garlic in Dutch oven over low heat 3 minutes. Stir in wine and Worcestershire sauce. Heat to boiling; reduce heat. Simmer uncovered, stirring occasionally, 10 minutes.

While onion mixture is simmering, cook and stir beef until brown; drain off fat.

Stir chili powder, celery seed, pepper, salt and cumin into onion mixture. Simmer uncovered, stirring occasionally, 10 minutes. Stir in tomatoes and beef; break up tomatoes with fork. Heat to boiling; reduce heat. Cover and simmer, stirring occasionally, 30 minutes.

Stir in kidney beans (with liquid). Heat to boiling; reduce heat. Cover and simmer 30 minutes. Uncover and simmer, stirring occasionally, 30 minutes longer.

Chili and Macaroni

6 TO 8 SERVINGS

1 pound ground beef
2 medium onions, chopped (about 1 cup)
1 medium green pepper, chopped (about 1 cup)
3 1/2 ounces uncooked elbow macaroni (about 1 cup)
2 teaspoons chili powder
1 teaspoon salt
1/8 teaspoon cayenne pepper
1/8 teaspoon paprika
1 can (28 ounces) whole tomatoes, undrained
1 can (15 1/2 ounces) kidney beans, undrained
1 can (8 ounces) tomato sauce

Cook and stir ground beef, onions and green pepper in 12-inch skillet until beef is brown and onions are tender; drain. Stir in remaining ingredients; break up tomatoes. Heat to boiling; reduce heat. Cover and simmer, stirring occasionally, until macaroni is tender, 20 to 30 minutes.

CHILI CON CARNE: Omit elbow macaroni. Cook uncovered until desired consistency, about 45 minutes.

Cincinnati Chili

1 pound ground beef
3 medium onions, chopped (about
  1½ cups)
1 tablespoon chili powder
1 teaspoon salt
1 can (16 ounces) whole tomatoes,
  undrained
1 can (15½ ounces) kidney beans,
  undrained
1 can (8 ounces) tomato sauce
1 package (6 or 7 ounces) uncooked
  spaghetti
1¼ cups shredded Cheddar cheese
  (5 ounces)

Cook and stir ground beef and about 1 cup of the onions in 3-quart saucepan until beef is brown and onions are tender; drain. Stir in chili powder, salt, tomatoes, beans and tomato sauce; break up tomatoes. Cook uncovered over medium heat until of desired consistency, about 10 minutes.

Cook spaghetti as directed on package; drain. For each serving, spoon about ¾ cup beef mixture over 1 cup hot spaghetti. Sprinkle each serving with ¼ cup cheese and about 2 tablespoons remaining onion.

Top with dollop of dairy sour cream and sliced hot chili pepper, if desired.

TO MICROWAVE: Crumble ground beef into 2-quart microwavable casserole; add 1 cup of the onions. Cover loosely and microwave on high 3 minutes; break up beef and stir. Cover loosely and microwave until very little pink remains in beef, 2 to 5 minutes longer; drain.

Stir in tomatoes; break up. Stir in chili powder, salt, beans and tomato sauce. Cover tightly and microwave 8 minutes; stir. Cover tightly and microwave until hot and bubbly, 6 to 9 minutes longer. Continue as directed above.

Taco Salad

1 pound ground beef
1 can (8 ounces) tomato sauce
1 cup water
1/2 teaspoon salt
1/2 teaspoon chili powder
1/2 teaspoon garlic powder
1/2 teaspoon onion powder
1/8 teaspoon cayenne red pepper
1 head lettuce, chilled
4 tomatoes, cut into eighths
1 cup shredded Cheddar cheese (about
   4 ounces)
1/2 cup sliced green onions (with tops)
4 slices bacon, crisply cooked and
   crumbled
1/2 package (10-ounce) tortilla chips

Cook and stir ground beef in large skillet until brown; drain. Stir in tomato sauce, water and seasonings; heat to boiling. Reduce heat; simmer uncovered, stirring occasionally, 15 minutes. Cool 10 minutes. Tear lettuce into bite-size pieces. Combine lettuce, tomatoes, cheese, onion, bacon and tortilla chips in large salad bowl. Pour warm ground beef mixture over salad; toss gently. Serve immediately.

Barbecue Salad

6 cups bite-size pieces Bibb, Boston or
   leaf lettuce
1 pound ground beef
1 large onion, chopped (about 1 cup)
1 bottle (14 ounces) ketchup
1 tablespoon white vinegar
2 teaspoons sugar
2 teaspoons dry mustard
1/2 teaspoon salt
1 can (1 3/4 ounces) shoestring potatoes

Place lettuce in large bowl. Cook and stir ground beef and onion in 10-inch skillet over medium heat until beef is brown and onion is tender; drain. Stir in ketchup, vinegar, sugar, mustard and salt. Cover and cook over low heat, stirring occasionally, 30 minutes. Pour warm beef mixture over lettuce; toss gently. Top each serving with shoestring potatoes. Serve immediately.

Mexican Salad

6 cups bite-size pieces Bibb, Boston or
  leaf lettuce
1 large tomato, cut into sixths
1 green pepper, cut into 1-inch pieces
1 cup shredded Cheddar cheese (4 ounces)
1 can (16 ounces) kidney beans, rinsed
  and drained
1 pound ground beef
1 small onion, chopped (about ¼ cup)
2 tablespoons chili powder
1 tablespoon beef stock base
¾ cup water
6 drops red pepper sauce
1 teaspoon cornstarch
1 tablespoon cold water

Combine lettuce, tomato, green pepper, cheese and kidney beans in large salad bowl. Cook and stir ground beef and onion in 10-inch skillet over medium heat until beef is brown and onion is tender; drain. Stir in chili powder, beef stock base, ¾ cup water and the red pepper sauce. Cook uncovered over low heat, stirring occasionally, 10 minutes. Mix cornstarch and 1 tablespoon water; stir into beef mixture. Heat to boiling, stirring constantly. Boil and stir 1 minute. Pour warm beef mixture over lettuce mixture; toss gently. Serve immediately.

Veal Patties with Pears

1 pound ground veal
¼ cup butter cracker crumbs (about
  6 round crackers)
¾ teaspoon ground allspice
½ teaspoon salt
¼ teaspoon pepper
1 egg
1 tablespoon margarine or butter
¼ cup slivered almonds
2 small firm unpared pears, cut into
  ½-inch slices
1 cup apple juice
2 teaspoons cornstarch

Mix ground veal, cracker crumbs, allspice, salt, pepper and egg. Shape into 4 patties, each about ¾ inch thick. Heat margarine in 10-inch skillet over medium heat until melted. Cook patties in margarine, turning once, until brown and no longer pink in center, 7 to 8 minutes on each side. Remove patties; keep warm.

Add almonds and pears to skillet. Mix apple juice and cornstarch until smooth; stir into skillet. Heat to boiling, stirring constantly. Boil and stir 1 minute. Pour sauce and pears over veal.

TURKEY PATTIES WITH PEARS: Substitute 1 pound ground turkey for the veal.

Veal Chow Mein

1 pound coarsely ground veal
2 medium stalks celery, sliced
1 medium onion, sliced
2 cups bean sprouts (about 4 ounces)
1 tablespoon soy sauce
1 can (10½ ounces) condensed beef broth
1 can (4 ounces) mushroom stems and
  pieces, undrained
¼ cup cold water
2 tablespoons cornstarch
Chow mein noodles

Cook and stir ground veal, celery and onion in 10-inch skillet over medium heat until veal is brown. Stir in bean sprouts, soy sauce, broth and mushrooms.

Heat to boiling, stirring occasionally. Mix cold water and cornstarch; gradually stir into veal mixture. Heat to boiling, stirring constantly. Boil and stir 1 minute. Serve over chow mein noodles.

Scotch Eggs

8 hard-cooked eggs, peeled
¼ cup all-purpose flour
1 pound bulk pork sausage
¾ cup dry bread crumbs
½ teaspoon ground sage
¼ teaspoon salt
2 eggs, beaten
Vegetable oil

Coat each hard-cooked egg with flour. Divide sausage into 8 equal parts. Pat one part sausage around each egg to cover. Mix bread crumbs, sage and salt. Dip sausage-coated eggs into 2 beaten eggs; roll in bread crumb mixture.

Heat oil (1½ to 2 inches) in 3-quart saucepan to 360°. Fry eggs, 4 at a time, turning occasionally, 5 to 6 minutes; drain. Serve hot or cold.

Canadian Pork Pie

1 pound ground pork
½ pound ground beef
1 medium onion, chopped (about ½ cup)
1 clove garlic, chopped
½ cup water
1½ teaspoons salt
½ teaspoon dried thyme leaves
¼ teaspoon ground sage
¼ teaspoon pepper
⅛ teaspoon ground cloves
Egg Pastry (below)

Heat all ingredients except Egg Pastry in large skillet to boiling, stirring constantly; reduce heat. Cook, stirring constantly, until meat is light brown but still moist, about 5 minutes. Prepare Egg Pastry.

Heat oven to 425°. Pour meat mixture into pastry-lined pie plate. Cover with top crust; seal and press firmly around edge with fork. (Dip fork into flour occasionally to prevent sticking.) Cover edge with 3-inch strip of aluminum foil; remove foil during last 15 minutes of baking. Bake until crust is brown, 35 to 40 minutes. Let stand 10 minutes before cutting.

EGG PASTRY

⅔ cup plus 2 tablespoons shortening
2 cups all-purpose flour
1 teaspoon salt
1 egg, slightly beaten
2 to 3 tablespoons cold water

Cut shortening into flour and salt until particles are size of small peas. Mix egg and 2 tablespoons water; stir into flour mixture until flour is moistened (add remaining tablespoon water if needed). Gather pastry into a ball; divide into halves and shape into 2 flattened rounds. Place one round on lightly floured cloth-covered board. Roll pastry 2 inches larger than inverted pie plate with floured cloth-covered rolling pin. Fold pastry into quarters; unfold and ease into plate.

Turn filling into pastry-lined pie plate. Trim overhanging edge of pastry ½ inch from rim of plate. Roll other round of pastry. Fold into quarters; cut slits so steam can escape. Place over filling and unfold. Trim overhanging edge of pastry 1 inch from rim of plate. Fold and roll top edge under lower edge, pressing on rim to seal securely.

Following pages: Canadian Pork Pie

Sausage Skillet Dinner

6 SERVINGS

1 pound bulk pork sausage
1 pound ground lamb
1 cup dry bread crumbs
1 cup finely chopped onion
1/4 cup snipped parsley
1/2 teaspoon salt
1 egg
1/2 teaspoon salt
1/4 teaspoon pepper
1/4 teaspoon dried rosemary leaves
1/4 teaspoon dried oregano leaves
1 can (6 ounces) eight-vegetable juice
1/2 head cabbage, shredded
*1 package (10 ounces) frozen peas and
   carrots, broken apart*

Mix pork, lamb, bread crumbs, onion, parsley, 1/2 teaspoon salt and the egg. Shape into 1 1/2-inch balls. Cook in 12-inch skillet over medium heat, turning occasionally, until brown, about 20 minutes; drain. Stir in 1/2 teaspoon salt, the pepper, rosemary, oregano and vegetable juice. Push meatballs to one side of skillet; add cabbage and peas. Heat to boiling; reduce heat. Cover and simmer 15 minutes, stirring occasionally.

Thai Pork and Pineapple

4 SERVINGS

1 tablespoon vegetable oil
4 cloves garlic, finely chopped
1 pound lean ground pork
1 to 2 jalapeño peppers, finely chopped
2 tablespoons sugar
1 tablespoon fish sauce
1/4 cup dry roasted peanuts, chopped
2 tablespoons snipped fresh cilantro
*1 small pineapple, pared, cored and cut
   into slices*
Snipped fresh cilantro

Heat oil in wok or 10-inch skillet until hot. Stir-fry garlic until light brown. Add pork; stir-fry until brown, 6 to 8 minutes. Spoon off fat. Add peppers, sugar and fish sauce; stir-fry 2 minutes. Add peanuts and 2 tablespoons cilantro; stir-fry 1 minute. Spoon pork mixture onto pineapple slices. Sprinkle with cilantro. Serve with hot cooked rice, if desired.

Italian Turkey Patties

6 SERVINGS

1 pound ground turkey
1/4 cup dry bread crumbs
1 tablespoon lemon juice
1 tablespoon olive oil
1 teaspoon salt
1 teaspoon rubbed sage
1/4 teaspoon pepper
3 slices provolone cheese or about 6
    tablespoons shredded mozzarella cheese
1 tablespoon margarine or butter
6 cups shredded cabbage
Salt and pepper to taste

Mix ground turkey, bread crumbs, lemon juice, oil, salt, sage and pepper. Shape mixture into 6 thin patties, each about 5 inches in diameter. Cut each slice cheese in half. Place half-slice cheese on half of each patty; fold patty over cheese. Carefully press edge to seal.

Heat margarine in 12-inch skillet over medium heat until melted and bubbly. Cook patties in margarine until done, about 4 minutes on each side. Remove patties from skillet; keep warm.

Cook and stir cabbage in drippings in skillet until wilted, about 5 minutes. Sprinkle with salt and pepper. Serve with turkey patties; garnish with lemon wedges, if desired.

Ground Lamb Kabobs

6 SERVINGS

6 pita breads (6 inches in diameter)
1 1/2 pounds ground lamb
1 medium onion, chopped
1 cup snipped parsley leaves
1 1/4 teaspoons salt
1/2 teaspoon coarsely ground pepper
1/2 teaspoon ground cumin
1/2 teaspoon paprika
1/4 teaspoon ground nutmeg
Vegetable oil
2 medium tomatoes, chopped
4 green onions (with tops), sliced
Plain yogurt

Split each pita bread halfway around edge with knife; separate to form pocket. Keep warm. Place lamb, chopped onion, parsley, salt, pepper, cumin, paprika and nutmeg in food processor; cover and process with about 20 on-off motions until mixture forms a paste.

Divide lamb mixture into 12 equal parts. Shape each part into a roll, 5 × 1 inch. (For easy shaping, dip hands in cold water from time to time.) Place 2 rolls lengthwise on each of six 14-inch metal skewers. Brush kabobs with oil.

Grill kabobs about 4 inches from medium coals, turning 2 or 3 times, until no longer pink inside, 10 to 12 minutes. Remove kabobs from skewers; spoon into pockets. Top with tomatoes, green onions and yogurt.

Lamb Meatballs

2 pounds ground lamb
1 tablespoon plain yogurt
2 teaspoons finely chopped gingerroot
2¼ teaspoons ground cumin
2¼ teaspoons ground coriander
1½ teaspoons salt
⅛ teaspoon pepper
1 teaspoon chili powder
½ cup vegetable oil
2 cardamom pods
1 stick cinnamon
1 cup water
¼ cup plain yogurt

Mix lamb, 1 tablespoon yogurt, the gingerroot, cumin, coriander, salt, pepper and chili powder. Shape into ovals, about 2 inches long and 1 inch thick. (For easy shaping, dip hands into cold water from time to time.)

Heat oil in 12-inch skillet until hot. Cook and stir cardamom and cinnamon 10 seconds; reduce heat to medium. Add meatballs. Cook uncovered, turning occasionally, until meatballs are brown, about 15 minutes; drain. Mix water and ¼ cup yogurt; pour over meatballs in skillet. Heat to boiling; reduce heat. Cover and simmer 10 minutes. Uncover and cook over medium heat until most of the liquid is evaporated, about 10 minutes. Remove cardamom and cinnamon. Remove meatballs with slotted spoon. Serve with basmati or white rice, if desired.

Stuffed Grape Leaves

1 jar (9 ounces) grape leaves
4 medium onions, finely chopped
1 teaspoons salt
3 tablespoons olive or vegetable oil
1½ pounds ground lamb or beef
⅔ cup uncooked regular rice
1 teaspoon salt
¼ teaspoon pepper
1 teaspoon snipped mint leaves or
    ½ teaspoon dried mint leaves
1½ cups water
3 eggs
3 tablespoons lemon juice
Lemon slices

Wash and drain grape leaves. Cook and stir onions and 1 teaspoon salt in oil until tender, about 5 minutes. Mix half the cooked onions, the lamb, rice, 1 teaspoon salt, the pepper and mint. Place rounded measuring tablespoon meat mixture on center of double layer of grape leaves. Fold stems over filling; fold in sides. Roll up tightly; place seam side down in 12-inch skillet or two 10-inch skillets. Repeat with remaining meat mixture and grape leaves. Add water and remaining cooked onions. Heat to boiling; reduce heat. Cover and simmer until tender, 50 to 55 minutes. Drain and reserve broth.

Beat eggs until thick and lemon colored, about 3 minutes. Slowly beat in lemon juice. Add enough water to broth from skillet to measure 1 cup if necessary; gradually stir into egg mixture. Pour over grape leaves. Simmer uncovered 10 to 15 minutes. Garnish with lemon slices.

Stuffed Meat Loaf

1¼ cups bulgur
1 pound ground lamb or beef
1 medium onion, finely chopped (about
    ½ cup)
1¾ teaspoons salt
⅛ teaspoon pepper
Stuffing (below)
2 tablespoons margarine or butter, melted

Heat oven to 350°. Cover bulgur with cold water; let stand 10 minutes. Drain; press bulgur to remove excess water. Mix lamb, onion, salt and pepper; add bulgur. Knead until well mixed. (Dip hands in cold water occasionally while kneading to moisten and soften mixture.) Prepare Stuffing.

Press half the lamb-bulgur mixture evenly in ungreased square pan, 8 × 8 × 2 inches. Cover with stuffing; spread remaining lamb-bulgur mixture evenly over stuffing. Cut diagonal lines across top to make diamond pattern. Pour margarine over meat loaf. Cook uncovered in oven until brown, about 40 minutes. Cut into diamond shapes; serve hot or cold.

STUFFING

¼ pound ground lamb or beef
1 small onion, finely chopped
2 tablespoons pine nuts (pignolia)
⅛ teaspoon ground cinnamon
Dash of ground nutmeg

Cook and stir all ingredients until lamb is light brown, about 5 minutes.

Lamb Patties with Summer Squash

4 SERVINGS

1 pound ground lamb
½ teaspoon garlic salt
¼ teaspoon pepper
2 small onions, cut into fourths
1 small green pepper, sliced
1 small summer squash, cut into ½-inch
  slices
1 tablespoon snipped fresh marjoram
  leaves or 1 teaspoon dried marjoram
  leaves

Mix lamb, garlic salt and pepper. Shape into 4 patties, each about ½ inch thick. Cook patties in 10-inch skillet over medium heat until light brown, about 5 minutes; turn.

Arrange vegetables around patties; sprinkle with marjoram. Cover and cook until lamb is done and vegetables are crisp-tender, about 8 minutes.

TO MICROWAVE: Prepare patties as directed above. Arrange on microwavable rack. Cover with waxed paper and microwave on high 4 minutes.

Arrange vegetables on and around lamb; sprinkle with marjoram. Cover with waxed paper and microwave 4 minutes; rotate rack ½ turn. Microwave until vegetables are crisp-tender and lamb is done, 3 to 5 minutes longer.

Ground Lamb Stroganoff

1 pound ground lamb
1 medium onion, chopped (about ½ cup)
1 can (10¾ ounces) condensed cream of chicken soup
1 can (4 ounces) mushroom stems and pieces, drained
½ teaspoon seasoned salt
¼ teaspoon pepper
½ cup dairy sour cream or plain yogurt
Hot buttered spinach noodles
1 medium carrot, finely shredded

Cook and stir ground lamb and onion in 10-inch skillet until lamb is brown; drain. Stir in soup, mushrooms, seasoned salt and pepper. Heat to boiling; reduce heat. Simmer uncovered, stirring frequently, 5 minutes.

Stir in sour cream; heat just until hot. Serve over noodles; sprinkle with carrot.

TO MICROWAVE: Crumble ground lamb into 2-quart microwavable casserole; add onion. Cover with waxed paper and microwave on high 3 minutes; stir. Cover with waxed paper and microwave until no longer pink, 2 to 3 minutes longer; drain.

Stir in soup, mushrooms, seasoned salt and pepper. Cover tightly and microwave 3 minutes; stir. Cover tightly and microwave to boiling, 2 to 3 minutes longer. Stir in sour cream. Cover tightly and microwave until hot, 1 to 2 minutes. Serve over noodles; sprinkle with carrot.

GROUND BEEF STROGANOFF: Substitute 1 pound ground beef for the lamb.

RED SPOON TIPS

Ground Meat History

Americans have always lived by the phrase "necessity is the mother of invention" and come up with creative uses for the materials on hand, so they were equal to the task of grinding their own meat. Cooks ground their meat with metal hand-operated grinders that often required a fair amount of elbow grease. Meat grinders were clamped to the kitchen table, and often the whole family was called into service to help the cook. Around the turn of the century, when the Hoosier cabinet's streamlined storage system revolutionized kitchens, a raised block for a meat grinder was standard issue on the Hoosier cabinet, and was welcome for saving wear and tear on the kitchen table, as well as allowing the meat grinder to stay in place safely. Today, even the greatest purist enjoys the ease and convenience of letting the butcher grind meat—it's also a more sanitary method.

Cooking Tips

If you have a problem fitting all your burgers into one skillet for a specific recipe, brown half. When all the burgers are browned return them to the skillet—they will have shrunk a bit, and the fit should be fine. Continue with your recipe as directed.

When broiling, grilling or microwaving ground beef, place meat on a rack—fat will drain away as meat cooks. If you are microwaving, be sure to use a microwavable, nonmetal rack.

When preparing soups, it is a little more effort, but certainly worth the time, to remove fat and trim calories. One quick method is to float an ice cube on top of the soup—the fat will congeal from the cold of the ice cube, and will be easy to skim off. You can also place soup in the refrigerator overnight—a particularly good step for many soups that benefit from letting their flavors sit and meld overnight. In the morning the fat will be on the top of the soup and can be easily removed.

Burgers are good candidates for make-ahead dinners. Spice and shape your burgers before the dinner rush—sitting in the refrigerator actually gives the seasonings a better chance to mingle with the meat and improve the flavor. Cover them lightly and refrigerate no longer than twenty-four hours. Avoid using wooden cutting boards and spoons as they can retain bacteria from the meat and pass it along to other foods.

When shaping ground meat, wear gloves if you have a cut or skin infection on your hand.

Guidelines for Buying Ground Beef

Buying ground meat is a breeze when you follow these simple tips.

• Check to be sure the package of ground meat isn't torn or damaged in any way, and is tightly wrapped.

• Look for meat that has a fresh, red color.

• Remember that ground meat achieves a "bloom" when exposed to air. Before ground beef is exposed to air, it has a purple tinge and the meat becomes red during packing. When you open a package of ground beef you may find that the outer layer has a lighter color, and the inside of the meat is darker. This is normal, and the meat is fine to use.

Ground Meat Storage Guide

It's important to understand how to store ground meat properly in the refrigerator and freezer so that you will always be cooking with fresh meat. Ground meat often goes on sale, and it makes good economic sense to stock up. Just follow these easy guidelines to ensure that your meat always tastes fresh and is safe to eat.

• Ground meat can be stored in the refrigerator in its original wrapping for up to 2 days in the coldest section of the refrigerator. If you don't use the meat after 2 days, rewrap the meat and store it in the freezer.

• If you have a large package of ground meat, divide it into smaller packets to make thawing time shorter.

• Layer ground meat patties between double sheets of freezer wrap so they separate easily, or freeze a single layer on cookie sheets, then transfer to freezer bags. This way patties won't stick together, and you can use as many as you need at one time.

• Make sure that your packages of ground meat are wrapped in moisture- and vapor-proof materials such as heavy-duty foil, plastic bags that seal tightly and tightly covered containers. Also make sure that you have pressed out the air from the package—this will help prevent freezer burn.

• Always label your packages, and write the date by which the meat must be used. Ground meat should not be stored in the freezer longer than 4 months. You can also add any special reheating instructions, or additional ingredients that will be needed before serving.

• When defrosting ground meat, transfer it to the refrigerator the night before you plan to use it so that it will be defrosted by the next evening. As a general rule, 1 pound of ground meat will thaw in approximately 24 hours.

• Never defrost ground meat at room temperature as it gives harmful bacteria the chance to grow and make the meat unsafe to eat.

• Use meat as soon as possible after defrosting—never refreeze defrosted ground meat.

Freezing Casseroles

Making two casseroles and freezing one for later can make the end of a hectic day an oasis of relief. Pop the frozen casserole in the oven and relax—just keep a few tips in mind.

• Slightly undercook meats, pasta and vegetables before freezing to prevent overcooking when reheating. When you prepare two casseroles—one to eat and one to freeze—set the freezer casserole aside a few minutes before it is fully cooked.

• Season lightly and add more seasoning just before serving. Pepper and some other spices become strong and bitter when frozen.

• Add crumb and cheese topping to frozen casseroles just before reheating.

• While thawing, sauces and gravies may appear curdled, but you can stir them smooth.

• If you want to bake a dish in a special casserole, but not tie it up in the freezer for several weeks, you can line the casserole with heavy-duty foil and cook the food in it. Cool the food quickly and freeze until set. Remove food in foil from casserole and wrap. To heat, unwrap and place in casserole.

- Casseroles take about 1 to 1½ hours to reheat—be sure to add more liquid, such as water, if the casserole looks dry.

- Casseroles should not be frozen longer than 2 months.

Below are four recipes that require some special handling in freezing and heating.

Stuffed Green Peppers

To Prepare: Follow recipe for Stuffed Green Peppers (page 43)—except stir in all the tomato sauce into the filling mixture; cover with aluminum foil but do not bake. Label; freeze no longer than 2 months.

To Serve: Bake foil-covered pan of frozen peppers in 350° oven until hot, 1 to 1¼ hours. Uncover, top peppers with Cheddar cheese slices, ketchup or chili sauce and bake 5 minutes.

Manicotti

To Prepare: Follow recipe for Manicotti (page 59)—except after filling shells, wrap securely in heavy-duty or double-thickness aluminum foil and label; freeze no longer than 2 months. Do not prepare tomato sauce.

To Serve: Unwrap frozen shells and place in ungreased baking pan, 13 × 9 × 2 inches. Prepare tomato sauce and pour over shells. Cover and bake until shells are tender, 1¾ to 2 hours.

Freezer Lasagne

To Prepare: Follow recipe for Lasagne (page 58)—except do not bake. Cover with aluminum foil and label; freeze no longer than 2 months.

To Serve: Bake foil-covered frozen Lasagne in 350° oven 1¼ hours. Uncover; bake until golden brown, 15 to 30 minutes longer.

Freezer Pasties

To Prepare: Follow recipe for Hamburger Pasties (page 24)—except do not prick tops or bake. Wrap each pasty securely in heavy-duty or double-thickness regular aluminum foil and label; freeze no longer than 2 months.

To Serve: Unwrap desired number of frozen Pasties and place on ungreased baking sheet. Prick tops with fork and bake in 375° oven until hot, 40 to 45 minutes.

	HAMBURGER (3 OUNCES)	LEAN GROUND BEEF (3 OUNCES)	EXTRA LEAN GROUND BEEF (3 OUNCES)
Calories	278	255	207
Riboflavin	11%	12%	12%
Thiamin	5%	5%	5%
Niacin	24%	26%	27%
Iron	12%	13%	14%
Zinc	28%	30%	31%
Protein	49%	52%	54%

All percentages refer to the U.S. Recommended Daily Allowances. Information in this chart provided by The National Live Stock and Meat Board.

Beef Basics

Ground meat has always been considered hearty, robust fare. While it certainly is filling on a cold, snowy evening or a gray rainy afternoon, it isn't just bulk-up food. Ground beef is a good source of protein and has other nutritive value as well. The chart above will give you an idea of the nutrition value of ground beef and how it can fit into your menu planning.

The Complete Hamburger

It's hard to think of a meal more popular and satisfying than a hamburger. Broiled, grilled, fried or baked, this simple patty has been elevated from a humble main dish to an American tradition. The hamburger traces its origins back to the Baltic countries where shredded and seasoned meat was eaten raw—also the origin of Steak Tartare. The dish found its way up to the town of Hamburg in Germany, where it was cooked and renamed. The hamburger made its way to America in the early 1800s and was featured in the 1904 Louisiana Purchase Exposition in St. Louis with two other all-time favorites— hot dogs and ice cream. In 1920 the first hamburger stand was opened in Wichita, Kansas, and America began its full-fledged fascination with the hamburger. Follow the information above to find the best ways to cook and serve your hamburgers.

Cooking Times and Techniques

To Bake: Place patties on a rack in a shallow pan. Bake in a 350° oven about 35 minutes for medium.

To Fry: Cook patties in large skillet over medium heat about 10 minutes for medium, turning frequently.

To Broil: Broil patties about 4 inches from heat 7 to 8 minutes on each side for medium, turning once.

To Microwave: Place 4 patties on a microwavable rack and cover loosely. Microwave on high 6 to 8 minutes for medium, rotating after 3 minutes.

To Grill: Grill patties about 4 inches from medium coals 7 to 8 minutes on each side for medium, turning once. Below you'll find tips for easy grilling.

Carefree Cookouts

Grilling outside always adds a special glamor and rich flavor to hamburgers, and their enticing smell draws most everyone to the grill. A hamburger cookout is an easy, informal way to cook a family meal or entertain friends, and with the following tips, you can relax and enjoy grilling your burgers as much as you do eating them.

▪ Keep a supply of long-handled grilling tools on hand, such as tongs, a fork and a basting brush, so you can keep your distance from the heat when cooking burgers.

▪ Use fire- and heat-resistant mitts when you have to work close to the grill.

▪ Use a pump-type water sprayer to control fire flare-ups. Follow manufacturer's instructions for flare-ups in gas and electric grills.

▪ A small grill pan is handy for heating sauces for burgers.

▪ Use an electrical charcoal starter to light your coals quickly and without odor.

▪ Cut down on cleanup by brushing the grill with vegetable oil before you begin grilling. This will help keep foods from sticking and leaving charred bits behind. After cooking, whisk or scrape any food particles off with a wire grill brush or crumpled handful of foil. Be sure to wear fire- and heat-proof mitts if the coals are still hot.

▪ Another cleaning tip: line the firebox of your grill with heavy-duty aluminum foil to make picking up the ashes easy, as well as to catch the drippings. Turn the foil shiny side up so it will also act as a heat reflector.

Serving Size

When buying ground meat, use the rule of thumb that ¼ pound of ground meat will serve one person. A pound of ground meat will feed 4 people.

Burger Bar

CONDIMENTS

Half the fun of eating a hamburger is in the "fixings," the condiments that go with the hamburger and that make each person's hamburger almost as personalized as fingerprints. Check the lists below for new ideas that can "beef up" your favorite burger.

Don't forget to have a selection of hamburger buns, toasted and untoasted, to house your delicious burger when it's cooked just right and loaded up with all your favorite fixings. You may enjoy a change from the standard hamburger bun—try English muffins, kaiser rolls, rye, pumpernickel or whole wheat bread.

SPICES AND HERBS

Use caution when seasoning—follow the adage "you can always add more, but you can't take it out." If you use fresh herbs rather than dried, you'll need to use about three times as many fresh herbs as dried for the same flavor.

Basil	Mace
Cayenne red pepper	Marjoram
Chili powder	Mustard (dry)
Cumin seed	Nutmeg
Curry powder	Oregano
Garlic	Paprika
Ginger	Parsley
Lemon pepper	Sage
Salt	Sesame seed
Pepper	Thyme

SAUCES AND TOPPINGS

Be sure to have several different toppings on hand when serving burgers, to please all tastes.

Barbecue sauce	Alfalfa sprouts
Blue cheese dressing	Avocado slices
Chili sauce	Bell pepper rings
Chutney	Cooked bacon
Horseradish sauce	Coleslaw
Ketchup	Onion slices
Mayonnaise	Pickles (sweet and sour)
Mustard	
Pickle relish	Shredded lettuce
Worcestershire sauce	Sliced mushrooms
	Tomato slices

Many people feel that a hamburger is positively naked unless it's topped with a slice of cheese, so have slices ready to put on the hamburger in the final moments of cooking. Try American, Swiss, Cheddar, Monterey Jack and mozzarella.

Special toppings from your own kitchen can be the perfect condiment for a hamburger. Whether a medley of onions or mushrooms and onions, your homemade barbecue sauce, a tart yet rich mustard butter, or other delicious butter, your family and friends will love these special toppings that are better than "store-bought." These toppings are terrific on hamburgers straight from the skillet or hot off the grill.

Broiled Onion Topping

1 tablespoon margarine or butter
2 medium onions, chopped (about 1 cup)
1/8 teaspoon ground nutmeg
2 tablespoons sour cream

Melt margarine in small skillet. Add onions; cook and stir until tender. Stir in remaining ingredients; spread on cooked patties. Broil 2 inches from heat until hot, about 1 minute.

Mushroom-Onion Topping

1 tablespoon margarine or butter
1 medium onion, thinly sliced
1 can (4 ounces) mushroom stems and
   pieces, drained
1/2 teaspoon Worcestershire sauce
1/8 teaspoon pepper

Melt margarine in small skillet. Add onion; cook and stir until tender. Stir in remaining ingredients and heat. Serve hot over patties.

Spicy Barbecue Sauce

ABOUT 3/4 CUP SAUCE

1/3 cup margarine or butter
2 tablespoons water
2 tablespoons vinegar
1 tablespoon Worcestershire sauce
1 teaspoon sugar
1 teaspoon onion salt
1/2 teaspoon garlic powder
1/2 teaspoon pepper
Dash of ground red pepper

Heat all ingredients, stirring frequently, until margarine is melted.

Barbecue Sauce

1 cup ketchup
½ cup finely chopped onion
⅓ cup water
¼ cup margarine or butter
1 tablespoon paprika
1 tablespoon packed brown sugar
½ teaspoon salt
¼ teaspoon pepper
¼ cup lemon juice
1 tablespoon Worcestershire sauce

Heat all ingredients except lemon juice and Worchestershire sauce to boiling in 1-quart saucepan over medium heat. Stir in lemon juice and Worchestershire sauce; heat until hot.

Mexican Casera Sauce

2 medium tomatoes, finely chopped
1 medium onion, chopped (about ½ cup)
1 small clove garlic, finely chopped
1 canned jalapeño pepper, seeded and
   finely chopped
½ teaspoon jalapeño pepper liquid
   (from jalapeño pepper can)
1 tablespoon finely snipped cilantro, if
   desired
1 tablespoon lemon juice
1½ tablespoons vegetable oil
½ teaspoon dried oregano leaves

Mix all ingredients. Cover and refrigerate in glass or plastic container up to 7 days.

Mustard Butter

¼ cup margarine or butter, softened
1 tablespoon snipped parsley
2 tablespoons prepared mustard
¼ teaspoon onion salt

Mix all ingredients. Spoon over hot burgers.

Sesame Butter

ENOUGH FOR 4 BURGERS

¹/₄ cup margarine or butter, softened
1 teaspoon Worcestershire sauce
¹/₂ teaspoon garlic salt
1 tablespoon toasted sesame seed*

Mix all ingredients. Spoon over hot burgers.

Garlic Butter

ENOUGH FOR 6 BURGERS

¹/₄ cup margarine or butter, softened
¹/₂ teaspoon paprika
¹/₈ teaspoon pepper
2 cloves garlic, crushed

Mix all ingredients. Spoon over hot burgers.

Herb Butter

ENOUGH FOR 6 BURGERS

¹/₄ cup margarine or butter, softened
1 to 2 tablespoons chopped fresh herbs
*   (basil, chives, oregano, savory, tarragon*
*   or thyme)*
1 teaspoon lemon juice
¹/₄ teaspoon salt

Mix all ingredients. Spoon over hot burgers.

*To toast sesame seed, spread in ungreased shallow baking pan; bake in 350° oven until golden brown, 5 to 19 minutes.

Serving Suggestions

You may have a package of ground meat in the freezer but be fresh out of ideas for how to use it. The section that follows will help you use the recipes in this book to plan meals for children, meals from different countries, meals to make ahead and meals for grilling. The Menus' section will give you ideas for easy entertaining that deliciously incorporates the recipes in this collection. In fact, after reading this section, you may wish you had more packages of ground meat in the freezer.

KIDS' FAVORITES

Favorite Burgers

Chili-Cheese Burgers

Taco Patties

Grilled Coney Island Burgers

Tacos

Souper Baked Sandwich

Hamburger Pizza

Sausage Burritos

Chiliburgers in Crusts

Sloppy Joes

Double-Cheese Hamburger Casserole

One-Skillet Spaghetti

Baked Macaroni with Beef and Cheese

Cincinnati Chili

Sloppy Joes with Potatoes and Onions

Chili and Macaroni

Beef-Vegetable Soup

Pocket Stew

Lasagne

ETHNIC DISHES

Scandinavian Hamburgers

Grilled Jalapeño Buffalo Burgers

Piroshki

Spicy Lamb in Pita Breads

Moussaka

Ground Lamb and Eggplant

Oriental Sandwich

Latin Meatballs

Baked Stuffed Papayas

Thai Pork and Pineapple

Stuffed Grape Leaves

Mostaccioli with Beef and Prosciutto Sauce

MAKE-AHEAD MEALS

Chiliburgers in Crusts

Piroshki

Lasagne (See freezer recipe, page 100.)

Scotch Eggs

Stuffed Grape Leaves

Stuffed Green Peppers (See freezer recipe, page 100.)

Manicotti (See freezer recipe, page 100.)

Hamburger Pasties (See freezer recipe, page 100.)

GRILLING GREATS

Burgundy Burgers

Favorite Burgers

Zesty Burgers

Chili-Cheese Burgers

Blue Ribbon Burgers

Grilled Hamburgers

Grilled Coney Island Burgers

Marinated Blue Cheese Burgers

Grilled Jalapeño Buffalo Burgers

Southwest Burgers

Grilled Teriyaki Burgers

Grilled Deviled Burgers

Menus

HAMBURGER COOKOUT

Favorite Burgers (page 7)
Potato salad
Sliced tomatoes with Bermuda onions
Corn on the cob
Chocolate chip cookies
Sliced watermelon
Milk and Iced Tea

CALORIE COUNTER'S MENU

Lamb Patties with Fresh Mint Sauce (page 53)
Parsleyed noodles
Green beans with lemon pepper
Wedges of melon
Meringue cookies
Skim milk
Mineral water

HEARTY WINTER DINNER

Lasagne (page 58)
Warm garlic bread
Crisp mixed green salad
Cannoli or Amaretti cookies
Cappuccino
Red wine

WARM WEATHER DINNER

Cold cucumber soup
Turkey Taco Salad (page 48)
Lemon sorbet
Limeade

COMPANY FARE

Canadian Pork Pie (page 87)
Sautéed zucchini and carrots
Hearts of palm salad
Rolls and butter
Chocolate mousse
Coffee and tea

INDEX

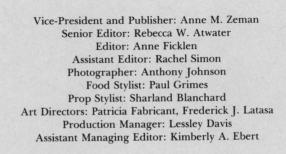
Vice-President and Publisher: Anne M. Zeman
Senior Editor: Rebecca W. Atwater
Editor: Anne Ficklen
Assistant Editor: Rachel Simon
Photographer: Anthony Johnson
Food Stylist: Paul Grimes
Prop Stylist: Sharland Blanchard
Art Directors: Patricia Fabricant, Frederick J. Latasa
Production Manager: Lessley Davis
Assistant Managing Editor: Kimberly A. Ebert